I'M POSSIBLE

I'M POSSIBLE

A Story of Survival, a Tuba,
and the Small Miracle
of a Big Dream

RICHARD ANTOINE WHITE

FLATIRON
BOOKS
NEW YORK

This is a work of nonfiction. Dialogue in it has been reconstructed to
the best of the author's recollection.

www.flatironbooks.com

Designed by Michelle McMillian

Library of Congress Cataloging-in-Publication Data

Names: White, Richard Antoine, author.
Title: I'm possible : a story of survival, a tuba, and the small miracle of a big dream /
    Richard Antoine White.
Other titles: Impossible
Description: First edition. | New York : Flatiron Books, 2021.
Identifiers: LCCN 2021026488 | ISBN 9781250269645 (hardcover) |
    ISBN 9781250269652 (ebook)
Subjects: LCSH: White, Richard Antoine. | Tubists—United States—Biography. |
    African American musicians—Biography. | LCGFT: Autobiographies.
Classification: LCC ML419.W413 A3 2021 | DDC 788.9/8092 [B] —dc23
LC record available at https://lccn.loc.gov/2021026488

Our books may be purchased in bulk for promotional, educational, or business use.
Please contact your local bookseller or the Macmillan Corporate and Premium Sales
Department at 1-800-221-7945, extension 5442, or by email at
MacmillanSpecialMarkets@macmillan.com.

First Edition: 2021

10 9 8 7 6 5 4 3 2

TO CHERYL WHITE AND

RICHARD AND VIVIAN MCCLAIN

Contents

PART III: PATHWAYS OF POSSIBILITY   191

I'm Possible

I button up my tux and the world shifts. For a short while, everything moves at half speed. I walk slowly. I sit slowly. I speak slowly. I conserve my breath. Buzzing into my mouthpiece, I walk onstage and am greeted by the plumage of red seats, soft and inviting. Slowly, quietly, the audience bubbles into the theater, which is aglow. They hush at the sight of us holding our instruments, flipping through the sheets on our stands, or closing our eyes—trying to get close to the music one way or another.

I play the piece in my mind, letting it unfurl just as I want it to when I put my lips on the brass mouthpiece of my tuba.

I inhale an epic breath and allow myself, fleetingly, to think, *I have made it.*

The lights dim. The crowd settles. The conductor raises his arms and the hall pulses, alive.

The harp; the piano; the woodwinds—flutes, oboes, clarinets, and bassoons; the strings—violins, violas, cellos, and bass; the percussion—snares, xylophones, bass drum, and timpani; the brass—trumpets, French horns, trombones, and tuba. All our voices become one. One powerful voice that draws everyone present into a whole other world of hope and passion, sadness and joy, and possibility.

. . .

People pay attention when you say, "I'm the first . . ." You know—the first in your family to go to college or the first woman to be president. In my case, I'm the first African American to earn a doctorate of music in tuba performance. And when I say that, people pay attention, and sometimes they assume that I'm a genius or that I'm special. Based on how my life began, I can see that my musical journey seems like a minor miracle, that even the fact of my survival is some kind of marvel. But the most miraculous part of my story is not me—it is the people who kept me from falling through the cracks, the people who saved my life. The people who cared enough to take me in, to teach me, to push me, to tell me something I wouldn't have otherwise known, and to challenge me to be better. I'm no different from the next person, although I do possess a profound belief in what is possible and a deep gratitude for how I came to be here.

The first time my life was saved was on the day I was born. My mom was seventeen. My biological father was nineteen—he got locked up before I was born, and when I arrived in the world, he wasn't there. I was born premature at Maryland General Hospital and weighed just over a pound. Richard McClain, the man who raised me, said he could put me in his hand and close it. He would tell me, "Boy, you had all those tubes hooked up to you—comin' out your nose, goin' into your mouth, and I would just feel so bad every time I went to go see you. Yes, sir. Sure glad you made it . . . mmm hmmmmm."

The second time someone saved my life was a few months later. I have a small scar just to the right of my navel, a flat keloid scar that's as much a part of my body as my little finger or my nose. I can't remember a time when it wasn't there, but I never knew where it came from. Richard McClain's son Ricky Jr. told me that when I was an infant, the McClain family got a call from someone in Sandtown–Pennsylvania Avenue—the neighborhood in Baltimore where I'm from—saying that there was a baby screaming in an abandoned building. Everyone knew that my mom had a baby and that she had alcohol problems, and no one wanted to call Child Protective Services on her, so they called the McClains. Ricky Jr. came searching for me. The house was just a burnt-out shell, and when he found me there was a mischief of rats swarming around, nibbling on my side. He shot at them—*Bam, Bam*—and they scattered, and he was struck with the fear that the shots would damage my hearing. It turns out my ears are okay.

To be honest, I have a great ear. I have my mom's ear—Cheryl could really sing, and she'd sing all the time. She introduced me to music and she also instilled in me a powerful sense of determination that carried me through all manner of trouble.

We didn't have an apartment or a room that we had a key to. There was no place with a lease in my mom's name. Sometimes we had shelter, but it was never a home. At the end of the day, I didn't know where home was. All I had was Mama, and from a very young age, I had a profound urge to protect her. Though I knew she had an illness, I believed that I could take care of her. But first, I had to find her. There weren't any tricks for that. I would simply search every place I could remember. *Oh, she might be in the park. Oh, she might be under the tree. Oh, she might be at this house or that house.* I'd search on an endless loop until I found her. Sometimes it would get dark before that happened and I would just crawl into an abandoned house and sleep there. That searching taught me perseverance. It taught me to keep working a problem until I solved it. Sometimes I feel like I do things the hardest way, but I never forget how to do them. I also have a tireless sense of optimism. I know that everything is possible.

I want you to read this story and feel like you are a superhero. I want you to read this book and dream big, impossible dreams. Looking at the beginning of my life, everyone would have thought it was impossible for me to survive, impossible for me to succeed, impossible for me to be who I have become. But here I am, standing on a stage, playing the tuba, living a happy life. I am possible. And therefore I know that anything is possible.

I am possible. You are possible. Everything is possible.

Part I
GROW GREAT

By the time I graduated from high school, my dream was to get an orchestra job. I didn't know that it is easier to get into the NBA than it is to get into a symphony orchestra. Your odds are even worse if you're African American. Less than 3 percent of orchestra musicians are African American. And while there might be thirty-two violins in an orchestra, there is usually only one tuba. Finding these jobs is like finding a needle in a haystack. But that's what I wanted. I wanted it so badly I could taste it.

I started professional auditioning in 1996, ten years after I began to play the tuba. To audition, you must be invited to play for the committee. When I tell you that I was invited to audition in Albuquerque for the New Mexico Symphony Orchestra, it sounds rather elegant. Maybe you're picturing a handful of musicians in their tuxes, so it is important that you understand that these weren't auditions of only the elite; they were cattle calls.

I scraped together money for the plane ticket, the overweight luggage fee, *and* the oversized luggage fee to fly my two tubas in their hard cases. I stayed with an old friend, Peter Landers, and slept on his couch.

The next morning when I showed up at the old church the orchestra was using for auditions, I was herded into the warm-up room with ten other tuba players who were all auditioning for the same job—and we were just the first batch. In an hour, another ten people would show up. The committee probably heard thirty or forty players that day. I drew a number from a big glass bowl just inside the door to see which batch of players I would audition with.

For a beat we all looked at one another, then the latches on our cases were sprung and the room exploded in a cacophony of sound. *Baaawp. Shamp. Shamp. Bo Bo Bo Bo. Bee. Bee. Be. Be. Beeee. O. OOO. OOOO.* People were running scales. They were fluttering their lips, buzzing into their mouthpieces, and emptying spit valves. The warm-up practice room was a flurry of sound and saliva and nervous energy.

I took a moment to put my heavier tuba by the door to the audition stage and returned to the *Baaawp Shamp Bo Be O* of the practice room. I learned that trick after having to walk to several auditions from the cattle room—down the hall, up steps, down steps, and around the corner carrying two tubas—only to sit down on the stage already out of breath.

Eventually, the audition proctor popped his head in the door. "Group two!" he called out over the pandemonium. Five of us moved toward the door, everyone lugging their two tubas. I carried my lighter tuba and followed the proctor slowly, focusing on my breathing. Sometimes the proctor would offer to carry one of the tubas, but even then they walk fast and I would appear onstage to play short of breath. So I learned to set the pace and walk stupid slow.

The auditioning room was a church pulpit. There was one chair and the excerpts were arranged on a music stand. A black curtain portioned the church in two. The screen was there so that the auditions were truly blind. The auditioner's voice was not allowed to be heard. Even their footsteps were not allowed to be heard. The church's floor was wooden and there was a carpet spread over it so the committee couldn't hear the click of women's heels or the squeak of sneakers. The committee didn't know the race or gender or age of anyone who played. There was only music.

I knew it was there to protect me, but I had the urge to see the screen come down. I wanted to see the faces on the other side when I, a 250-pound Black man from Baltimore, broke their hearts with the sound of my tuba.

I waited at the side door as the first person in our auditioning group played. The church was quiet. He whispered a question to the proctor, the proctor announced it to the auditioning committee seated on the other side of the screen, and the committee gave their answer, then the tubist lifted his instrument.

When it was my turn, I played the first excerpt, then the second. After the third one, a voice behind the curtain said, "The committee would like the candidate to play the excerpt again, focusing on the rhythm."

I thought to myself, *You're telling me I suck, but do it again.* My nerves were sparking so that I couldn't think about what they wanted me to change. I played it again, and it was identical to the first time.

The auditioning committee couldn't see me and I couldn't see them, but sometimes I could hear them—a cough, a snicker.

"Thank you," someone said dismissively.

Over a decade of work and a thousand dollars to travel here, and within five minutes I'd played all five excerpts and was sent on to a room where I sat waiting to hear if I was good enough. One by one the other musicians filed in and then the proctor came back and announced the names of the musicians who would advance to the next round. He didn't say my name.

I had gone from homeless on the Baltimore streets to studying for my doctorate in tuba at one of the most competitive music programs in the world, but I still wasn't on the level. I thought about a piece of advice Professor Edmund Cord gave me right after my very first orchestra audition, in Indianapolis: *If you want to get to where you've never been, you've got to start doing the things you've never done.*

I went back to work—practicing five to six hours a day. I was going to bring that screen down. I was going to win an orchestra spot. But first, I had to grow great.

On the Move

The water fountain rose above me. I eyed it and in one swift move hoisted myself up on the stone ledge, then let my toes dangle until I felt the smooth, cool pedal. Arms trembling, I gulped water and scrubbed the stray drops into my face.

Mama wasn't at the park. She wasn't at the light blue row house with the peeling paint where she'd been hanging out the night before. And she wasn't at the big tree on Riggs Avenue either. I'd woken up alone curled between a tree's roots early that morning after having fallen asleep listening to Mama laughing with Rocksey as they passed a brown bag between them.

My stomach growled. The last thing I'd eaten was half an egg sandwich yesterday morning when I had found Mama on the marble steps in front of a gray-painted brick building with boarded-up windows.

I started up Carrollton Avenue. Maybe Mama would be looking for me at Grandma Bernice's. In the morning we were like a magnet to a refrigerator. We found each other, always.

From an open window, the smell of bacon hit me. I eyed the trash basket. No one was looking, so I scanned the nest of bags and cups and greasy wrappers. Last week I'd found a box of chicken wings with the wing tips fully intact and I'd sucked the meat off each of those bones until they were clean. But on this morning, I found something better beside the basket, a coin. And then another! I snatched them up and tucked them deep in my pocket where I had a few others. Maybe there'd be chicken gizzards today.

I heaved open the door to the corner store. A blast of cool air hit me, and I was drawn in by the glitter of candy stacked in the plexiglass treasure box, the cashier towering over it.

He leaned over the counter. "Can I help you?" I knew enough to understand that he was really asking, *Do you have money?*

"Have you seen my mom?"

"Not today."

Grandma Bernice, my mom's birth mother, lived down the block from Grandma Emma, my dad's mom. I walked past the big black fire escape and the little shoe store and decided to knock on Grandma Emma's door. Maybe my cousins would be heading to the playground in the lot behind Grandma's place.

Aunt Thumberlina answered the door.

"Have you seen my mom?"

"Naw, Ricky. She ain't here."

I hovered in the door, craning my neck to see if my baby uncle Pedro—Grandma Emma had him real old and he was younger than me—was playing inside, but she shooed me away. "Boy, you smell. Get on out of here."

My uncles Glen and James, aka Goo Goo, were in the alley, and my cousin Jeffrey was laughing and yelling as he ran ahead of them into the playground behind Grandma's house.

"Hey!" I called happily.

Goo Goo turned around and sang out, "Snotty nose, stinky clothes. Go find your mother."

Grandma Emma stuck her head out the door and hollered, "Leave that boy alone, or I'll hit you upside the head."

I waved to her as I started to chase Jeffrey down the street. But the neighbor lady marched down the white steps. "Come on over here and let me wipe your nose."

She launched a tissue attack as I tried to squirm free. "Sit still," she said.

"It's fine. It's fine," I said, pushing her hand away.

By the time she was satisfied, Jeffrey was out of sight and my stomach was rumbling. I made my way to Bernice's; Mama wasn't there either so I headed back toward the tree.

There were a few men playing dominoes at a fold-up card table set up in the cool shade of the big branches. The bones clacked on the plastic. A small group was gathering, but Mama still wasn't there.

I started hunting for coins. At night, people were always hanging out here—drinking, smoking, getting high, then tripping, falling, and dropping money. *Tink. Clink. Clink.*

I lay on the drainage grate and swooped my arm into the dark hole, brushing against cold sludge. Nothing. Some kids would crawl into the drain, but I was too scared. My luck came from the coins that hadn't been washed down or what I found in the gutters. As I walked along, I bulldozed my big toe through the gutters—pushing aside leaves, a cherry-red soda can, a slimy scrap of wax paper—and then: the silver shimmer of a coin. My stomach rumbled again.

On Riggs I nearly smacked into the man with the jacked face. The skin stretched over his eye, nose, and cheek was weirdly shiny and smooth. It folded and bunched like the melted cheese that had hardened on day-old pizza. My heart skittered.

I darted down the block, dodging traffic on Fremont Avenue, and arrived at the community center, where they sometimes gave away free box lunches that had a piece of fruit, a bologna and cheese sandwich, milk, and juice. But no one was there today and I was pretty sure I had gizzard money, so I climbed through the hole in the fence. There, its high red walls looming above me, was Lafayette Market.

There were a few horses tied up outside. Sometimes I'd see them on the streets of Sandtown, pulling the carts as tall Black men sat up front calling out "Watermeloooon" or "Get your crabs." It was a Baltimore thing. Inside Lafayette Market, a swarm of people moved from one stand to the next. There was a horse cart with a mound of watermelon, another full of pints of strawberries, bright red and sweet-smelling. One cart was painted red and filled with buckets of crabs, their blue and red claws scrabbling up the sides.

I was like an ant underfoot. Invisible. A hip knocked into me and I stumbled into some lady's bag of groceries. I looked up to see who I'd hit and when I looked down again, *CRASH*, I bumped into a man heaving a big box. I lifted my chin, trying to figure out where I was. I spun in a circle—where was the chicken stall? All I saw were legs and bags bulging with food, and hands. Hands holding car keys and grocery bags, hands that were smooth and brown with brightly painted nails, or wrinkled and ashy. Hunger poked at me. *Don't get lost today.* I found the side door I'd come through and closed my eyes. All I had to do was walk straight, go right, then straight, and then *BOOM*: chicken.

I opened my eyes and saw a pigeon stutter from one rafter to the next. Refocusing on the task at hand, I set out. Straight. Right. Straight. I dodged legs and strollers with kids bigger than me.

At the chicken booth, I stood on the gray cement looking up, trying to stretch myself taller. The lady working came out from behind the counter and put her hands on her knees. "Hey, kid."

I held out my palm displaying the jumble of coins. She pecked about until only a few blackened pennies were left. She didn't ask me what I wanted. I'm pretty sure the money did the ordering, but I never left without chicken. She came back with a bag full of fried chicken gizzards. Hot. Crunchy. Salt, pepper, ketchup on the tongue.

I was ready to play. Leaving the market, I sidestepped a pile of horse droppings and strolled to the playground behind Grandma Emma's, slowly chewing a gizzard.

"Ricky's it!" Jeffrey yelled as I chased after them, my little legs churning through the grass and my hands still clutching the bag, grease spots spreading along the bottom and sides where my fingers met the warm meat.

I tagged Rodney, who lived on the block between my two grandmothers, and he smiled shyly. His mom was always offering me sandwiches and he had her sweet disposition.

"Why you carrying that chicken around, Ricky?" baby uncle Pedro asked.

I shrugged. But there was no way I was setting that bag down. The chicken stayed with me. It stayed with me when I ran to base. It stayed with me when I sat on the swings. It stayed with me when I went back to Lafayette Park—aka the Square.

There was Mama. She was tall. Her big curls made her even taller. I slipped onto the bench beside her and handed over the greasy bag, grinning. She eyed me suspiciously.

"Who gave you that?"

"No one."

"How'd you find that?"

"I bought it."

"Where'd you get the money? You begging?"

"No. I found it."

Mama knew I wouldn't lie. She dipped her fingers into the bag and closed her eyes as she chewed.

Staring up at the clouds, I started thinking about my name. Longing for something different, after a while I said, "I wish my name was Anthony."

"Well, you know your name is Anthony. Antoine is a form of Anthony. Richard Antoine White is your name." And then she kissed me on the forehead and said, "I love you, baby." She handed me the bag, but I was full, so I just tucked a piece of chicken under my tongue in case there wasn't food later.

From that day on I always announced my full name: Richard Antoine White.

Mama and I walked everywhere. If we needed to go to the east side of town, we walked. If we wanted to go to the west side of town, we walked. Walking with Mama was halfway between being dragged across town and flying. Sometimes I'd imagine myself as Road Runner, my legs moving so fast they were invisible.

When Mama told me, "Rocksey said we could stay at her house," we walked fast, occasionally breaking into trots and full-on runs so awkward that I ended up stumbling on the cracked sidewalk.

"Come on, boy. Come on, boy. Let's go."

We went, with a trash bag bouncing over Mama's shoulder.

Rocksey and Mama were best friends. They would sit around playing cards or watching their stories—*The Young and the Restless* or *Days of Our Lives*—on the TV with the hanger perched on top. They passed a green pack of Kool 100s between them until the air was thick and gray and one of them said, "Let's go get a hit." A hit meant they were going to the big tree to get a swig from the bag. Someone under the tree always had a brown paper bag with the tip of a bottle poking out—Thunderbird or Mad Dog 20/20.

My mom and Rocksey had been pregnant at the same time and she had a daughter, Danielle, whom I called Hot Chicken. She had a lot of *toys*. While Mom and Rocksey watched their stories, I played. Hot Chicken had a water toy with a transparent tank and two white buttons that you pushed to squirt the rings up over the poles. I shook it. *How are the rings in the water?* I turned the whole thing upside down. I pushed the buttons and tiny bubbles emerged. *How does it work?* I tugged at the blue top. It didn't come off. I pried at the blue base. It didn't budge. I shook and pushed that plastic until I felt it give, and a flood of water washed the bright little rings out onto the vinyl floor.

Rocksey was not happy.

She was even less happy when a couple weeks later a few dollars went missing. She and Mom had been drinking all afternoon and the big ash-tray sat between them with a gang of butts that had been smoked down to the filter and stubbed out. The pack of Kools was empty.

"I need a fug. I'm gonna run to the store." Rocksey fumbled around on the table for her money.

"Ricky. You take that dollar that was sitting here," she said, more accusation than question.

"No, ma'am."

"Don't lie to me. Did you take it?"

We went round in circles until Mama took up for me. "He wouldn't lie. If he did take the money, he would tell you."

"Then how'd he get those chicken wings?" Rocksey demanded.

"I found money." I'd found enough to take to Lafayette Market. This time the smiling woman had taken all the coins in my hand and given me a box of chicken wings.

"Ricky wouldn't take your money."

"No. I know I left the dollars right here."

Mama drew herself up to her full height. "I'm telling you, Ricky does not lie. If he did it he would say he did it." Every word was a knife.

Rocksey cut her eyes at me but spoke to Mama, "Get your shit and get out."

Mama shoved our stash of clothes into trash bags, and then we were on the move. One bag slung over her shoulder, the other slung over mine.

We half-flew down the block. My arm went tingly from the weight of the bag. I wanted to put it down for a minute but didn't want Mama to get mad. I tried to shift the weight around to get the feeling back in my fingers. But after another minute I couldn't, and the black plastic slipped from my grasp. Mama kept walking. I couldn't heave the bag off the ground again so I started dragging it.

"Come on, boy!"

My yellow T-shirt poked out of a hole that had opened near the cor-ner. I tried to force it back in and Mama spun on her heel and hit me upside the head. Tears stung my eyes. She grabbed my hand and I trailed behind her, the garbage bag trailing behind me.

"Just leave it. We gotta go," Mom told me when I looked back, tears skimming my cheeks. I abandoned my bag of belongings.

"Come on!" But I wasn't fast enough. "I said, come on, damn it," she said like I wasn't tough enough or strong enough.

"I'm trying," I muttered, my jaw tight. I willed the tears to stop. We walked on.

By the time Rocksey found the money and realized I wasn't lying, we were long gone.

Mornings were story time.

Mom scooped me off the floor where I'd been sleeping and laid me on the couch beside her. Her friend was asleep upstairs and we just lay there in the early morning light, whispering.

When Mama was still and holding me close, I could talk to her about anything. Her strong arm was warm against me when I asked about my dad. But no matter how many times I asked, I always got a real short answer: "Your dad got in trouble. He got life."

Then the conversation would move along, like a father in prison was no big thing.

If I couldn't have my father, then maybe a brother. "I wish I had a little brother. Then I wouldn't be alone."

"Well, I can't have any more kids," Mama said softly, then steered the conversation away from family. "Today, we're going to go to Social Security." She ran her fingers up and down my back, and I closed my eyes and listened. "I'm gonna get some food stamps. We're going to run over to Ms. DeAnne's to do the ironing. Then we're going to go talk to Aunt Regina about staying with her until I can get us our own place. I'm working on that, baby. We're gonna have our own place."

We started making moves. First, we'd head down to Social Security. It was a long walk followed by a long wait. I'd shift from one foot to the other and try not to fidget so much that Mama would get annoyed. Then, food stamps in hand, we walked all the way back to Sandtown, to Dolphin Street, to Ms. DeAnne's.

On the front steps, Mama held my hand in hers. It felt strong and warm.

"Hey, Dee," Mama said. Ms. DeAnne pulled Mama into a big hug and squeezed my cheek.

Ms. DeAnne was always giving Mama odd jobs and letting us stay with her. They'd been friends forever and she'd say, "Cheryl, I got some ironing to do."

Mama stood singing at the ironing board, the iron hissing, a can of starch nearby. "Lovin' you is easy 'cause you're beautiful," she sang as I spun a top across the floor and watched it dance off the wall back into the center of the living room floor.

She moved from Minnie Riperton to Grease, and when she got to "Greased Lightnin'," I joined in: "Greased lightnin', go greased lightnin'." We grinned at each other.

Ms. DeAnne was older and the house smelled like old people, but she was real nice. She gave me Popsicle sticks and rubber bands and I made a switchblade, which was a lot more fun than eating the starchy chalk-like mess she'd give me to snack on. It would coat my mouth and stick between my teeth, so I'd have to dig around with my finger, popping bits off the teeth at the back of my mouth.

When the ironing was done, Ms. DeAnne pushed a few dollars into Mama's hand and said, "Honey, we'll see you soon."

"Thank you." Mama slipped the money in her pocket, and when she looked at me there was a shine in her deep brown eyes. "Let's go get something. Whatchu want?"

"A cookie!"

My mom could navigate the heck out of a dollar. In the penny candy store, she walked up to the high counter and said to the Asian man behind the bulletproof glass, "Give me two fugs, a bag of chips, a cookie, and a soda." She'd slide the dollar through the slot and tell me to pick out some penny candy, and I'd get a mountain of sweets in their crinkly cellophane wrappers.

It was a feast.

Aunt Regina's was busting at the seams when we arrived. Her husband, Big Country, who owned a yellow car we would sometimes ride around in, swung the door open and revealed a tornado of children. Aunt Regina raised eight kids. Tracey giggled at Mama and me from behind Big Country's massive legs. He was just a little younger than me, and he had a tiny scar by his eye. Mama told me he'd gotten burned playing with candles, but I'm not sure if that was the truth or a lie grown-ups tell to keep kids safe.

Mama hugged Regina and set her bag of Thunderbird on the table alongside a pack of Kools. Aunt Regina smiled. Her smile was always a little bigger when we didn't come empty-handed.

Tracey had warmed up and he and I ran around with my cousins playing hot butter bean.

"Hot butter bean, come and get your supper!" an older cousin called out from a bedroom on the second floor, and we scattered, hiding in bathtubs, closets, behind doors, and under tables. We ran and ran until we collapsed in front of the TV and watched whatever was on.

Regina had been messing around in the kitchen, and when she called her kids to the table, Mama came over. "Ricky, come on. We're goin' over to Bernice's."

When Uncle Pork Chop answered the door at Bernice's, I hung back behind Mama and held her hand tight. Bernice was in the kitchen frying chicken and the house smelled of oil and Marlboro cigarettes.

Another brother, Lamb Chop, was sitting on the brown, plastic-covered couch watching TV with Grandpa Ike.

"Hey, Cheryl," he said, and nodded at me.

My uncles were big men and my mom was tall too, and everything in the room felt close. They moved to the dining room table and played cards for a bit.

"Whatchu up to?" Pork Chop asked.

"Did a little ironing for DeAnne today. Saw Regina and them."

Bernice came out with a plate of food. Other aunts and uncles drifted in and out. They'd take turns playing cards and smoking on the stoop. I stretched out on the floor beside the plastic-covered couch and my eyes fluttered shut.

I woke up to raised voices.

Mama's leg bounced fast; Pork Chop spoke sharply. Then she called out to me, "Ricky. Let's go."

"Cheryl, why don't you just let him stay here?" Bernice said.

"Naw, he's coming with me. He's my kid." When Mama stood, she looked tall and fierce. I scrambled to my feet trying to mask a yawn.

Pork Chop's voice was winding up, getting louder. "You're going to hurt this boy. You need to get your shit together. This is no way to raise a kid." He took a step between me and Mama.

"Mind your business. I take care of my own goddamn son."

"Oh, I'm gonna mind my business all right. You need to get it together. This ain't right." Pork Chop's eyes were red, his voice raw.

"You better get out of my face." Mama reached her hand out for me, but I was too scared to push around my uncle in the room crowded with furniture and people. I could hear my aunts' and uncles' voices, but I didn't know what they were saying. I didn't take my eyes off Mama and Pork Chop, who was getting closer to her.

"I ain't getting out of your face. This needs to be addressed. Your drunk ass needs to get it together. What you gonna do about it?"

"I told you to get out of my face."

"You ain't taking that boy outta this house."

"You better get outta my way." Mama's fingers drummed against her thigh.

"I said, you ain't taking that boy." Pork Chop loomed real close to her. Mama pushed him.

"What?!" He shoved her back.

She balled up her fist and swung at his head. "This is my son and he's going with me."

He knocked her, hard. She tripped on a chair and hit the floor. When she scrambled up, he slapped her hard enough that blood started dripping from her nose.

I wrapped my arms tight around her leg.

I hated Pork Chop.

Mama slammed the door behind us and we picked our way down the marble steps where a couple of my aunts sat smoking. Cigarettes burnt down to the butts lay in a constellation of ash.

It was a relief to be out in the night air.

A while back they'd kicked Mama out of the house and I'd had to stay the night. She was outside screaming, "Let me in!" Banging on the door as Pork Chop yelled at Mama to go away and Lamb Chop yelled at me to get upstairs.

I stood there, refusing to move.

"Come on. Give me my son." Her voice was ragged.

"Go upstairs," Lamb Chop said again.

"I don't want to," I said. "I want to go with my mama."

"Go!" he roared. I charged toward the door and he held me, easily, as I flung my fists and feet at him.

Then Bernice held me tight and took me upstairs. I could still hear Mama at the door. I knew they'd talk bad about my mom and the next morning they'd kick me out.

"Go on and find her," Pork Chop would grunt.

But on this night, I was right beside Mama. Her whole body was coiled tight, anger coming off her like heat. Mama's breath rattled in her chest. She was digging in her pockets for her asthma spray. *Puff. One. Two. Three. Puff.* Her breath quieted.

Then we were on the move. We headed to the tree so she could get a squig. I stubbed my toe on some broken cement. She whipped around fast and popped me upside the head. "Dumbass, come on!"

The night was on the bubble.

We met with her friends over at the tree. All the other kids were home. There was a radio playing. Then someone said, "That's my jam," and began to dance, and soon people were grooving.

"Give me a squig," Mama said, holding her hand out to a dude with an afro. He handed her the brown paper bag and she took a sip, and then it just never ended.

The squig turned to, "Give me a couple bucks, so I can get my own."

"Ricky, wait here while I run to the store." And she and the afro dude walked off together.

I wanted to go with her but knew better than to argue. I watched as her white ruffled shirt disappeared into the dark.

I worried that she wouldn't come back. But having to find Mama in the morning was a whole lot better than the nights when she went home with someone and would take me with her. If I'd fallen asleep, she'd scoop me up and carry me to whatever row house we were going to sleep in. She was real strong but if she was drunk, we would fall and I'd wake up banging onto the sidewalk. Most of the time I'd trudge behind her and the dude into some strange house. One night I awoke to the sound of my mom crying out. The dude was on top of her. It didn't feel right. I started kicking, drumming my heels into the small of his back—he didn't so much as pause. He started grunting and Mama was making a small whining sound that flipped a switch in my brain. I wanted him off my mom. I stood on the bed, like I was King Kong, pounding my fists into his back. Zero effect. Absolutely nothing. Then it was over.

Mama rolled toward me and said, "Go to sleep."

But on the night that I sat under the tree waiting, she reappeared. She'd cleaned the blood off her face and seemed looser, like some of the anger at Pork Chop had rolled off. I sat with my head on my knees, watching her. For a while it was all right, just a nice buzz she floated on top of. She would laugh and I would lean in close.

Earth, Wind & Fire's "Shining Star" came on and Mama started to sing along: "Shining bright to see / What you could truly be," and then she grabbed my hands and we swayed together under those big branches.

The song ended and a man with a scraggly beard and a gold chain came up to Mama.

"How you doin', Cheryl? It's good to see you."

"Hey. Whatchu doin' tonight?"

"I'm gonna go get a drink maybe."

"All right, well, let's go together."

"I heard some folks was getting together around the corner. Let's go around there." Then Mama picked her way over the tree roots, wobbling this way and that. I stayed close.

"Come on," she called to the others, then fell.

I crouched beside her. "You okay, Mama?"

I tried to help her up, but I was so small and she was so big. Scragglybearded gold-chain dude appeared and Mama leaned into him as she limped back to the group.

I found a scrap of cardboard and laid it between two roots.

In the morning I looked for Mama, feeling the dew on my bare feet.

A Visit to Buckingham Palace

It was starting to get colder. Mama and I walked from DeAnne's on Dolphin Street, where we'd spent the night, to Grandma Bernice's place.

"Mama, I thought you said we were going to get our own place," I said, a little out of breath from trying to keep up with her long strides.

"We are. I'm working on that," she said, and kept walking. We were going to Bernice's to get ready for Sunday dinner with the McClains.

Even though Bernice was Mama's mother, when Mama was a toddler she went to live with Richard and Vivian McClain. Back in those days family and friends helped each other out, so Mama's godparents became her parents. Richard and Vivian only had one child themselves, Ricky Jr., and were able to provide for Mama and adopt three other children. Bernice already had at least eight other kids and it was just too much—the house was full and it was hard to put food on the table.

Visiting Mr. Richard and Ms. Vivian was a big deal. It meant washing up real good, putting on our best, cleanest clothes, and wearing shoes.

I hated wearing shoes.

I never wore them because they never fit. I would just step out of them and if the shoes came off, they stayed off. Once I almost got frostbite in a winter storm because I went barefoot through the snow. Sometimes, if I'd been teased enough about being shoeless, I would find shoes in a dumpster, or in the trash outside the cobbler shop near Grandma Emma's house, and I'd put newspaper in the toes and try to wear them. This was a trick Mama used when we got shoes from shelters or thrift stores. If we found shoes, they were *never* the right size. You can't do anything with too-small, so you do too-big and put newspaper in them.

Before we set out for the McClains', Grandma Bernice fussed over my bare feet. She brought out an old pair of shoes that belonged to one of my cousins. They were giant. She handed me sheets of newspaper and I stuffed them into the tips of the shoes.

My feet looked basketball-player big and I kept tripping over them as I clomped around. I walked outside and Grandpa Ike, who was sitting on the front steps, just started laughing.

Mama smelled of baby powder and I breathed her scent in as we walked, freshly scrubbed and hand in hand, to catch the bus down Pennsylvania Avenue to Park Heights, and then walk another stretch to the house.

Mama prepped me. "Ms. Vivian and me don't get along. But I want you to be nice. If something happens you stay close to me. We're going to try to stay long, but we may not."

As we got closer, she grew quiet and slowed down.

Wow.

It was the nicest house I'd ever seen, with a porch and stone columns, and a yard so big that none of its sides touched any other house. It had cream stucco walls and green trim around the windows. They had a garage that was like a whole other house. An American flag fluttered in the breeze.

Ms. Vivian answered the door. She was a big, strong-looking woman who towered over me. Her hair was short and looped into big brown curls. She looked at Mama and frowned and said, "You ought to do better." But then she turned to me with a big grin and swooped down, scooping me into a hug. She planted kisses on both my cheeks and the top of my head. "Baby Ricky! Come in."

Their living room had a lush red carpet that made me want to take my shoes off and dig my toes in. There was a wall made entirely of glass tiles that I could see my reflection in, and an enormous cabinet filled with china and glasses with gold rims. One of the McClains' sons, Robert, showed me the basement. It was a house in and of itself to me. There was a bathroom, a work area, a stove, a refrigerator, and a bar—a full bar with stools. Robert had a bedroom down there. Then he took me back up to the first floor and showed me the sprawling kitchen with a nook where people could sit and eat, that was totally different from the dining room where you could *also* sit and eat. I was sure we would be eating at the big fancy table. It was set—a tablecloth and glasses and pretty plates in front of every chair.

Robert showed me Ms. Vivian and Mr. Richard's room, and then he showed me Grandpa Archie's room, Archie was Vivian's dad. Then Robert took me up to the third floor where Angie and Ricky Jr. each had bedrooms. Mama had had a bedroom up here when she was a girl. In the row houses I'd seen, everyone had a small room and the doors were always shut. Here, everyone had giant rooms and the doors were always open. Everyone was free to go in everybody's room. Nothing was locked.

I couldn't believe my mom had grown up in such a fancy house. It may as well have been Buckingham Palace.

I tugged on Mama's arm. "Mama, why don't we live here?"

"We can't live here."

I couldn't let it go. "Why not?" I asked as I stared at my reflection in the glass tiles. Mama didn't say anything; she just shook her head from side to side and shot me a look that said, *Hell no.*

In the giant kitchen, Vivian pushed candy and cookies into my hands until I couldn't hold any more. Whatever I wanted, the answer was yes.

"Could I please have some milk?"

"Sure, baby."

"Could I please have a cookie?"

"Sure, baby."

"Could I please play in the backyard?"

"Sure, baby."

Angie, the youngest of Richard and Vivian's three adopted daughters including my mom and Rhonda, smiled and walked me out back. I followed her shyly until I saw the vast expanse of grass that stretched behind their house. I ran a few circles around the yard, my legs moving so fast I thought I might lose control. Then I climbed the gate that encircled a firepit and swung back and forth, the black hinges squealing.

Grandpa Archie smiled, a perfect denture smile. He was light-skinned, like his daughter, and had thin gray hair and kind eyes. He sat at the painted red picnic table whittling a piece of wood. He'd made his living as a carpenter and he worked the piece of wood into a thin arrow with smooth edges.

From the gate, I spied a sliding board. Well, maybe it wasn't a sliding board exactly, but I was sure I could make a slide out of it. There were two metal cellar doors to the basement, set right under a window. I clambered up the door and slid down on my knees, then I raced back and slid down on my bottom. *Wheeeee!* I giggled and laughed until Vivian appeared.

"You're going to hurt yourself, boy. Get down and come inside. It's time to eat."

Seated at the table were Richard, Vivian, and their son Ricky Jr.; their adopted kids—Angie, Rhonda, and Robert; and my mom and me. The other kids were all so old, in high school or college. College—that seemed exotic to me. I didn't really know what it was for, but I did know that no one I knew went to college.

Angie pinched my cheeks and asked me how I was doing. Ricky Jr. got me to count.

I showed off what I could. I'd started prekindergarten at Harlem Park that year, though I didn't go very often. But I knew my alphabet and numbers and I could spell my name: "R-I-C-H-A-R-D W-H-I-T-E."

When we sat down to dinner, Vivian bowed her head.

"Close your eyes, Ricky," Mama whispered. I wasn't sure what was happening. I squinted my eyes shut, and then peeked. Everyone sat around the table, heads bowed.

"God is great," Vivian prayed, arms extended. "God is good. Let us thank him for our food. Amen."

Then everyone began to eat. There were potatoes thick with butter and salt and a delicious meat that I could pull tender strings from. They wiggled as I dangled them from my fingers. I giggled.

Vivian said, "Baby Ricky, use a spoon to eat."

"Okay." I went right back to eating with my fingers.

Vivian leaned over. "Let me cut that pot roast for you." She wielded her knife and fork, leaving a plate full of bite-sized pieces, then placed the spoon in my hand.

I set the spoon down and pulled another string from the pot roast. It melted in my mouth as I wiped my hands on my clothes.

Vivian gave me a stern look and held up her napkin, showing me what to do.

But the peas, man, I was not about the green peas. So every so often, when I was sure no one was looking, I slid one under my plate. Slick.

When Mama started clearing the plates, an avalanche of peas spread across the tablecloth.

Ms. Vivian gave me a withering look. "Boy, you eat those peas. This is food. We don't waste no food around here."

Everyone's eyes were on me.

Mama stepped in. "He doesn't want to eat that. Don't make him eat that."

"He's going to eat his vegetables. The boy needs his vegetables." Ms. Vivian fixed her eyes on me. Mama fixed her eyes on Vivian.

I leaned over and sucked a pea off the table.

In one swift motion, Vivian stood and smacked me upside the head. "You ain't no damn animal. You're gonna pick those peas up," she said, so that I knew there were no two ways about it.

I picked up the first pea and chewed it slowly, letting the sweetish green mush dissolve. I ate every single one of those peas off that table.

Mama and Ms. Vivian disappeared into the kitchen. Grandpa Archie called me over and snuck a peppermint into my hand. Then Mr.

Richard sent me into his room to find the box of oatmeal cream pies on his dresser. Boy, the sweet chewy cookie, the squish of icing—that was the greatest thing I'd ever tasted.

Then Mama erupted out of the kitchen screaming, "We ain't comin' back," and grabbed my hand as she moved toward the door.

That night we slept at Bernice's. I lay in Mama's arms and she whispered, "You're gonna be somebody. I know it. You know, things are hard, but you're gonna be somebody, baby. You're my star."

At the end of every day, whether I was washed or not, it was always me and Mama. I don't remember having a bear or blanket or anything; I clung to Mama. If Mama said she loved me, or she said something good, man, I held on to that like you wouldn't believe. The other thing I clung to was my name. If someone asked me, "Who are you?" I never just said "Ricky." Or "Baby Ricky." Or "Richard." I announced myself like I was staking a claim to something: "My name is Richard Antoine White. I was born May 17, 1973."

3

The Blizzard

That winter, everything changed.

There was a fierce storm whipping across Baltimore. The furious wind gusts stole the air, leaving nothing for me to breathe in. The flakes were coming so fast I couldn't see to the end of the block. Cars were covered. There was so much snow, the police were driving the blue-and-yellow Blue Ribbon bread trucks around. No one was outside. The whole world was white and quiet.

I'd been looking for Mama since I'd woken up in the cold of a boarded-up row house. I'd slid the loose boards away from the window and climbed up and started on my circuit. Mama wasn't at the corner store. She wasn't under the big tree. She wasn't at Dee's house. The Square in Lafayette Park was a blank field. It called to me—I was tired and I imagined lying in the soft snow and letting it blanket me as I drifted to sleep. But I had to find Mama.

My feet felt heavy. My legs felt heavy. I made it to Mosher Street. The fire escape just before Emma's house was mounded in snow, a strange skeleton against the red brick.

I banged on the door. I shouted, my words making clouds in the air. No one answered. The wind picked up, whipping icy snow into a swarm that stung my cheeks and nose.

I trudged down to Grandma Bernice's house. I could see a light on in the window. I used all my might to get someone to open the door. I pounded until my fists hurt. I screamed. No one appeared.

I didn't know where to go. I didn't know where Mama was. I didn't know if she was okay. But I was so tired. I just wanted to lie down.

Please, one of these doors open.

I forced myself to push along. Six houses down, between a pink row house and a red one, I saw the blue-gray building that Rodney lived in with his family. The door to the vestibule was open. I crawled in and fell asleep.

I woke up in a yellow room, in a bed, under a pile of blankets, with warm tea and food. There was a big scuttle about whether to call the authorities.

Rodney's mom said, "We've got to call somebody."

Rodney piped up, "Ms. Bernice is up the street. We could take him there. Or Ms. Emma is his daddy's people."

His mom didn't answer right away. Then very quietly she said to herself, "Maybe we should call the police."

Fear zinged through me.

The police didn't arrive, but Grandma Bernice did, and she was a storm of worry. "Lord, this don't make no sense. What are we gonna do?"

For a minute no one said anything. "Cheryl can't take care of the boy."

More and more adults were coming in, their voices ping-ponging over me as I held the mug of tea Rodney's mom pressed into my hands and kept refilling. The warmth spread from my hands into my bones.

Mama arrived. She kissed me and stroked my face. Her eyes were puffy and she talked to me quietly. I'd seen her angry. I'd seen her indignant. I'd seen her worried. But I'd never seen her afraid.

Bernice's voice got fierce and Mama seemed to shrink down. "This is so irresponsible. The boy could've died, Cheryl."

She didn't say, *I got this.* She didn't call out, *Come on, Ricky, we leaving.*

She didn't grab my arm and march me out. She just sat there real small, like all the fight had gone out of her.

Ms. Vivian and Mr. Richard came in and everyone talked. It was too much for me to keep up with. I was tired and just lay back and closed my eyes. Police. Authorities. Custody.

Then Ms. Vivian and Mr. Richard said goodbye and told me they'd see me real soon. Mama came back with Grandma Bernice and bundled me into my coat and shoes, and Mama carried me back to Bernice's place, where I'd pounded on the door with all my might the day before.

Nobody said much. Soon Bernice and my mom were fighting again and Mama left without me. She didn't come back that night. She didn't come back the next day either. I'd never spent so long without her.

"Ms. Bernice, do you know where Mama is?"

Instead of shooing me out the door and telling me to go and find her, Bernice just said, "Don't worry, Ricky. You gonna stay here for a bit."

She gave me clean clothes and I went to the upstairs bathroom to wash up.

One day Lamb Chop had a bag of cherries. I asked for one and he handed me the shiny fruit. I bit into the sweet, red meat, juice dribbling down my chin.

"Can I have my own bag?"

Lamb Chop guffawed and handed me another cherry.

I shooed a fly away. The grown-ups kept on talking in hushed voices and I sucked on the pit until every last scrap of fruit was gone.

One spring morning, Bernice saw one of the neighbors out washing their steps. Soon she had me out front scrubbing her steps with a bucket of water and Ajax and a scrub brush. It was contagious; it had become a step-cleaning day and kids and women up and down the block were scrubbing their marble steps until they glowed. Washing away the salt and mud that had encrusted everything over the winter.

When I was done scrubbing, Uncle Phillip sat down. He was the only grown-up who really talked to me about what was happening. I understood that Mama wasn't coming back and that I was going to stay with Richard and Vivian. That seemed all right. I remembered Buckingham Palace. The yard, the porch, the wall full of shiny glass glinting at me. The oatmeal pies! I missed Mama, but she wasn't here, and I certainly wasn't going to miss Bernice and them.

Uncle Phillip said, "Richard gonna come get you. What kind of car you think they gonna have? They gonna have a Cadillac? A Lincoln?"

I just shrugged.

"They gotta big house, right?"

I nodded.

"They're rich, right? It's gonna be great for you. You can go to school. You gonna eat every day. These are good people and they have a lot of money."

"But what about Mama? We gonna get her?"

Phillip acted like he hadn't heard me. He grinned and said, "And you gonna have your own bag of cherries."

When Mr. Richard came to get me a few weeks later, there was no tearful goodbye with Bernice or Uncle Phillip or Pork Chop or Lamb Chop or anyone else. No well-wishes, no goodbye at all. I was sitting on the front steps of Bernice's house alone with my trash bag of clothes. I'd never carried my trash bag of stuff anywhere without Mama.

Richard pulled up in a green Buick and waved his wiry arm at me. He didn't get out of the car. I just heaved my bag onto the back seat and climbed in.

I didn't look back.

4

Supermarket Wonder

Weird things happened as soon as I arrived at Richard and Vivian's house. First, they told me to call them Grandma and Granddad. Next, I was given my own room. I'd never had a room before. The third floor of their house had three bedrooms—Angie's room was the room on the left. Ricky Jr.'s room was on the right. My room was the open space in between. It wasn't really a room and nobody else wanted it, but it was mine, and they put a bed right there in it for me.

Then, there was bath time. I'd never been washed up by an adult. Vivian filled up an enameled metal bowl with water and lathered up a dark blue washcloth until there was soap everywhere—foaming out of the cloth, filling up the white bowl, and coating my scrawny body. I squirmed and she scrubbed, everywhere from the back of my ears to my behind and down to the skin between my toes.

"Boy, you filthy. Where does all the dirt come from?" she said as the suds turned gray. I hated the rough scratch of the washcloth and how she lifted and arranged my limbs to get at all the crevices, places that had *never* seen soap before.

Finally, she judged me clean enough and dried me off, squirting Keri lotion out of the big white bottle with blue writing and rubbing it into my skin until all the ashy bits shone. Her fingers worked fast, smearing

Vaseline over my face and scooping hair grease out of an orange-and-black can, rubbing it into my scalp and hair and brushing it out. My scalp screamed.

She handed me pajamas; they were light blue with perfect white buttons all down the front and they smelled good. "I sleep in these?" I asked Grandma as I slipped my arms into the long-sleeved button-down shirt.

She smiled and turned down the sheets in Grandpa Archie's room, right across the hall from Grandma and Granddad. He was away for a few days and they wanted me close so they could check on me.

I lay in bed and fumed. I missed my mother. Grandma was just the mean lady who screamed at my mom. She was the mean lady who took me away from my mom. She was the mean lady who wouldn't even let me see my mom. She was the mean lady who made me wash my butt and wear weird clothes to sleep. That's all she was.

Everything felt itchy and wrong. I kicked off the covers. I tried lying on one side and then the other. Then I crept out of bed, stripped off the pajamas, and put on my dirty clothes. I stretched my blanket between the bed and the chair in the corner to make a little tent and crawled underneath to fall fast asleep on the cool floor.

"Ooouuuuise!" Grandma's given name was Vivian Louise Wright, and Granddad sometimes called her by her nickname, Ouise. "You got to come get the boy! He's not well!" Granddad cried out in the night.

Grandma came running and they both stood in the doorway, staring at me.

"Boy, I thought you were sick. What you doing?" Granddad asked with a heavy Southern accent.

"I'm sleeping."

"What is all this?" He gestured to my tent. "Looks like some kind of ventilation tent."

"The boy is just sleeping," Grandma said calmly. "He is just comfortable on the floor and in his dirty clothes."

I curled back up on the floor and went to sleep.

The next morning in the kitchen nook, Vivian set down a warm bowl of oatmeal with brown sugar and cinnamon and a pat of butter cutting yellow rivers across the top. I ate it and it softened the ball of anger that was still roiling in my belly.

After breakfast I wandered past the wall of glass tiles. In each of them I found myself—someone I recognized.

"Hey, I know you," I said, and climbed up on a dining room chair for a better view. The chair was upholstered in white fabric and covered in thick plastic that crinkled beneath my knees.

I peered into one of the silvery squares. "I see you," I said softly, then smiled. I stared at myself for a while, making my eyes big and then squinting them shut. I struck some superhero poses, pointed and stuck out my tongue, and shot a cool look over my shoulder.

Moving close to a small glass square I whispered to myself, "I don't know these people. I ain't gonna talk to these people." My breath fogged the glass. "It's just you and me, buddy."

Soon I was having full-on conversations. They made me feel less lonely.

I may have been lonely, but I was never hungry. In the McClain house there was food, copious amounts of food, and Grandma expected you to eat all of it. Waste was not tolerated.

A few days after I first arrived, Grandma took me grocery shopping. The store was bright, with high ceilings and wide aisles, and filled with color. She lifted me up into the shopping cart and I swung my legs as we glided along the shiny white linoleum floors.

"What do you want?" she asked.

I looked at her dumbly as we passed mountains of bright red tomatoes, a mound of red onions, a wall of bananas. Then there was a pop of orange.

"Carrots!" I had always marveled at how Bugs Bunny gnawed carrots in a flash.

"You want carrots?"

I nodded and Grandma tossed the carrots in the cart. I was beginning to get the idea. "Grapefruit?" I asked.

"What? Grapefruit?" She pointed to giant pale oranges.

"No. Grapefruit cereal."

"Oh, Grape-Nuts?"

"Yes, ma'am."

I had seen commercials for Grape-Nuts and I wanted to feel the crunch.

When I got home, I chewed on a carrot like Bugs. *Nasty.* In the morning, instead of oatmeal I had Grape-Nuts. *Disgusting.* Over the next week Grandma made me eat those nasty carrots every day and that disgusting cereal every morning until the entire box was gone.

I had never had this quantity of food and I'd never been forced to eat anything, other than those peas that Grandma had made me eat. Even when I loved the food, I couldn't always eat it all and I always wanted to save some of it. Bologna on toasted bread was my favorite sandwich. So after lunch one day, I slid a sandwich off the plate and put it in my pocket.

Grandma and Granddad exchanged a look. I thought Grandma was going to yell, but she spoke to me gently: "You don't have to do that. This is yours. If you're hungry later I can make you another one."

Yeah, right, I thought. *Okay. I'm just gonna take this one with me.*

But Grandma didn't lie. I never went hungry. There was always food in their home. She made sure I could help myself. Right from the start, they began teaching me to be independent. They poured milk from the gallon jug into a jar and placed it on a shelf that I was able to reach so that I could get my own milk.

Even more amazing, before Grandma went to work for the day, she'd take some meat out of the freezer in the basement and set it out to thaw; when she got home, she put her apron on and got to cooking. I'm talking roast chicken and potatoes; chopped liver and onions; egg noodles and chicken with tomato sauce; her favorite, meatloaf; and my favorite, smothered pork chops and rice with gravy. Every night was a feast. But all I really wanted was Mama.

One sunny day I was running around the Harlem Park schoolyard at recess when I saw Mama at the fence. I pressed my fingers through the space in the wire and she touched them with her own. The world tilted.

"Ricky. Don't tell anyone you saw me. But, I had to tell you that I love you."

"I love you too, Mama. I wanna come with you."

"Naw, baby. You stay with the McClains and be good. You have to behave. These people are going to give you a better life." She looked over my shoulder.

"I don't care. I just want to be with you."

Tears burned my eyes and rushed down my cheeks. Snot ran out of my nose. She squeezed my fingers.

"They can give you a place to live. They can give you food and clothes."

"I don't want any of it. I just want you."

Her big brown eyes turned red and she began to cry. She dug the heels of her hands into her eyes, pushed the tears off her cheeks, and leaned toward me. Quietly she started singing, "Greased lightnin', go greased lightnin'." I joined her, our voices pushing together into one sound.

"You don't tell them you saw me today. Okay?"

I nodded.

"I love you. You be good, baby."

Mama had given me instructions, and I wasn't gonna let her down.

5

House Rules

I tried to be good, but I didn't always succeed. There was so much to learn.

I was living with strangers and it didn't help that they passed me off to other strangers. Even though Grandma and Granddad had taken me in, I had to finish the school year in Sandtown at my elementary school, Harlem Park, so during the week I stayed with a friend of Richard and Vivian's, Aunt Minna.

But one of the first weekends after I'd moved into the McClain home, I spent the weekend at Aunt Minna's too. That Sunday, Aunt Minna, her grandson Kenny, and I walked across a little bridge to get to church.

I'd never been in a church before. I just followed whatever Kenny did. I stood when he stood and I opened my mouth when he did, but I just pretended to say the words to whatever prayer or song was being said or sung. *La, La, La, La, Laaaaa, La, La.* I must have done okay, because Aunt Minna reached over and handed me a dollar. I gave her a little smile.

Soon a plate full of money came around. I took a handful and stuck it in my pocket. *Free money. Wow, this is church? This is nice.*

When we got home, Kenny marched up to his mom. "You won't

believe what he did. He took money from the oooofffffeeeering plate," he said with glee in his voice. "The whole church was looking at him. Check his pockets."

Aunt Minna drew crumpled dollar bills from my pockets. "Where did you get all this money from?"

"They were giving it away."

"Giving it away? Boy, you stole from the offering?"

"No. They gave it to me." *They had put it in my hand!*

"You ain't see, everybody else NOT takin' money out?"

I had no idea how to answer that.

"Why do you think I gave you the dollar?"

"Oh." I had no idea I was supposed to put the dollar in. My eyes got hot and started to sting.

"How could you be so stupid?"

I started to cry. Then we marched back to the church, and I had to give the money back and apologize. But I didn't really understand. It had been offered; I had taken it.

I'm from the streets. I grew up in survival mode. But despite my survival instincts, I almost killed everyone in the McClain house. I climbed under my bed and began playing with fire.

I pulled the little matches with red tips out of the box one by one. Swiping each stick against the strike pad, I marveled at the wisp of smoke and the sharp smell, willing each one to break into a bright flare. I struck and struck until finally there was the satisfying scrape, the smell of sulfur, and the whispering *whoosh* of fire. The small flame danced and jumped and suddenly a string on the bottom of the bed caught fire. I blew it out and lit another match. Scrape. Sulfur. *Whoosh*. Fire. Another string lit up. The flame rushed up the string and leapt to another and another. I couldn't put the little fires out.

I crawled out from under the bed and hid in my sleeping bag. There was yelling and scrambling, but I just kept my head tucked into the dark, warm bag.

Angie shouted, "Wake up. There's a fire in the house!"

Uncle Ricky Jr., who had been sleeping, burst into my room calling out, "Ricky! Where's Ricky at?"

I didn't say anything and he ran out. There was a chorus of voices from downstairs calling my name. Angie and Grandma and Granddad and Grandpa Archie were all screaming for me. Uncle Ricky ran back into my room and threw water on the bed and took a big blanket and smothered the fire. The house was filled with smoke.

I coughed and Uncle Ricky cried out, "I got him." He opened the sleeping bag and said, "Boy, you could have killed everybody in the house." Then he swept me up in his arms and carried me downstairs, where everyone had gathered in the kitchen.

When the smoke cleared, Grandma lit the stove. "Come here, boy." I hesitated, but there was nowhere else to go. She held my hands over the flame long enough that I knew I'd never mess with fire again.

Then I had to get buck naked and I got whipped with a belt. Everyone got a turn—Grandma, Granddad, Angie. I was screaming and dancing. But when it was Ricky's turn, he just pretended to beat me. I never played with matches again.

At the McClains', there were rules. Never play with fire, I mastered. But others were more challenging. I was used to roaming free. I did what I wanted when I wanted. So when I told Granddad I was going out to play and he said, "Come in when the lights come on," I bristled. *What are you talking about?* I thought. *I'm going outside. I'll be back when I'll be back.* But if I came in after the lights came on they would take things away—toys or TV time or, worse, there would be no outside time the next day.

There were rules *and* there were chores. Right away Grandma expected me to sweep the floor and make my bed. Pretty soon I was washing dishes—there was a green metal stool with three steps that I climbed up to reach the sink—and I was supposed to take out the trash.

One bright afternoon, I ducked under the picnic table and it became a spaceship that rocketed me off into the expanse of the universe. When

I returned to earth, I launched myself at the firepit gate and swung back and forth.

Grandma was hanging the laundry up on the line and called out, "Quit it, Ricky." And then, before I'd even had time to climb down, she added, "And go in and take out the trash. Didn't I tell you to do that after breakfast?"

When I didn't answer her, she persisted. "Ricky. Didn't I tell you to take out the trash before you went outside to play?"

In fact, she had told me to take out the trash as I guzzled milk, but I'd thought, *What do you mean, take out the trash? That's not my trash.*

She was revving up. "You can do when you want to do, you just don't want to. In my house . . ." *Why is she always saying that? What does that even mean, "You can do when you want to do"?* But I kept quiet and just let her rant.

The whole time, Grandpa Archie watched silently.

A few days later Grandpa Archie and I were sitting side by side in the yellow kitchen nook beneath the hanging stained glass lamp eating slices of peach, which he cut with his pocketknife and soaked in half-and-half.

We heard Grandma getting her car keys in the pantry near the back door and he leaned in close. "Robert-Richard." He was always mixing up our names. It was easy to do: Granddad was Richard Sr., and he had two sons, Robert and Richard Jr., whom they called Ricky, and now I was in the house too, so they called me Baby Ricky. On top of that, I called Richard Sr. "Granddad" and Vivian's dad "Grandpa Archie." I can see how that could be confusing. Names were a sign of respect and love and the confusion of our names somehow highlighted all the ways in which we were connected, even if it wasn't by blood.

Names aside, Grandpa Archie said under his breath, "You're going to just take the trash out before she says so, okay?"

I remembered my promise to Mama and hoisted up the black trash bag and maneuvered it through the garage to the big trash can outside.

When I sat back down Grandpa winked at me.

In the McClain house there were rules, chores, and also routines—so I started to know that I *would* eat and *when* I would eat, that I *would* sleep and *where* I would sleep, and that the McClains would be there every day when I woke up and each night when I lay down.

Sliding Board Lessons

I snuck up behind Grandpa, who was hunched over his bowl of peaches.

"Boo!" I hollered.

"Boy, you better stop scaring me like that," he said, clutching his hands over his heart.

I'd grown close to Grandpa Archie. He was quiet and steady and my best friend. If the bogeyman were to come in, I'd run to him. We watched baseball in his room and ate peppermints. When he nodded off, I'd quietly lug the brown plastic stereo-in-a-suitcase into his room and tenderly lift the case's lid, meticulously unwrap the cord, place the two speakers on either side of the case, and pull my favorite record out of its sleeve. Then, I'd set the needle down ever so gently and jam to "Macho Duck." Each time the song ended, I lifted the needle and moved it back to start the song over. As Grandpa lay on his bed snoring, I dipped my fingers into the bowl of tiny, colorful candies that looked like M&M's. I'd sort them by color and try to detect different flavors, but they were all peppermint.

"Baby Ricky, go ahead and get into the station wagon. We need to pick up a few things for school," Grandma called over a song, "Welcome to Rio." Normally, if something interrupted my Disney dance party I was annoyed, but I loved the red Pinto with the little silver horse on the front grill. I'd sit in the back and tumble around with every turn and curve of the car. It was my private playground.

September had rolled around and I was about to begin first grade. The McClains had enrolled me in the school near them, Cross Country.

We pulled into the wide, gray stretch of parking lot at Kmart, and Grandma asked me to help her remember what section we'd parked in. The store was all lights and big aisles overflowing with crisp pants, bright shirts, and brand-gleaming-new shoes.

We glided along the shiny white floors to the kids' section and Grandma said, "Get what you want."

My eyeballs must have bugged out of my head because she smiled and gently pushed me toward the clothes. "Pick out jeans, pants, two pairs of tennis shoes. Go on, pick out whatever you want."

I couldn't believe it. There were endless racks of shirts and stacks of pants. Colored? Or blue jeans?

Dizzy, I finally grabbed three pairs of jeans.

"Okay, well, how about we pick a couple pairs of different colors?" The cart started filling. There were blue jeans. Black and khaki pants. Shirts in yellow, orange, green, and pink. Vivian helped me try everything on. I was very small and finding things that fit was hard.

In the shoes section they had metal things to measure your feet. When I set my foot in one, nestling the heel into the curve at the back, the metal felt cool and comforting. Vivian knelt down and checked where my big toe met the silver lines.

She taught me how to find my shoe size printed on the side of the box. I was eyeing a pair of fresh white high-tops with a little check mark printed on the side. *I can't have these*, I thought. But Vivian just said, "If you want them, you can get them. But you gotta pick a regular pair too."

"What's a regular pair?"

"They are the low ones. You see, these are high-tops, these are low-tops. But you should get one of each if you want."

I caressed the shoes before setting them in the cart, which was filled with more clothes than I'd ever owned all put together. A knot started to form in my stomach when I thought about having to pay for all this.

But Vivian just said, "Okay. Now, let's go down there and get your school supplies." She whipped out a list of things I was supposed to have out of her purse. A ruler. Pencils. Five notebooks, each a different color. A box of crayons. An eraser. The list went on and on and she breezily tossed each item into the cart, occasionally asking me what color I preferred. When she marched up to the checkout, I dragged behind, worried about who was going to pay for all this. Certain that the woman at the cash register was eyeing me, I tried to make myself invisible as she rang every item up.

When the mountain of stuff was in bags, Vivian paid for it all without blinking. I remembered exactly where the car was parked and put my hand in hers as we walked to the car.

On the first day of school, Vivian made sure I looked sharp. She wiped the sleep out of my eyes, made my face shine with Vaseline, tied my shoes in double knots, and wished me a good day. Then Angie walked me to Cross Country Elementary.

"Bye, Baby Ricky," she called as I trotted through the steel doors into the squat brick building.

This school was different from Harlem Park, even though my teacher, Ms. Smith, had the same name as my Harlem Park teacher. From day one she began teaching me new things, including that there's a difference between being stupid and just having never been taught.

One of the things I hadn't been taught was how to read. I was in first grade, but when Ms. Smith called me over to the reading nook to have me read aloud to her, my stomach churned and a line of gobbledygook stretched across the page.

I enjoyed a lot of things about Cross Country Elementary. During quiet time, I loved sprawling out on the squishy mat that stretched across the floor. I'd lie there wishing that I'd had that mat on the streets of Sandtown. But the best part of school, by far, was recess. I raced out to the playground and there, looming above me, sun glinting off the metal, was the most magnificent sliding board I had ever seen. There was a silver ladder that rose up to the top of the slide, which swirled down to the ground. It was beautiful.

I had seen sliding boards before, but they were always the kind that shot straight down to the ground. I had never seen a curvy sliding board.

I plowed through the other kids, pushing my way in front of the boys and girls lined up. I scrambled to the top and pushed a kid off the ladder. "My turn," I cried out.

I zoomed down the slide, leaning into the curves and shooting off the bottom onto my behind. Gleefully, I ran right past the crying kid whom I'd pushed off the top into the crowd at the bottom of the ladder. Ms. Smith was looking down at me, arms akimbo. "We don't push people."

I just wanted to ride the sliding board.

Ms. Smith pulled me aside and said, "Look, you can ride the sliding board as many times as you want, but you have to stand in line."

"Why?" I asked, gazing up to the top of the magnificent metal structure.

"Because everybody has to get a turn. You have to share. The sliding board belongs to everybody."

I understood. Besides, there were other battles to wage.

Grandma ironed everything. My pants were starched stiff, my shirts smelled of laundry detergent and fresh air. She hung our clothes outside to dry on a clothesline with old wooden clothespins. One morning I put on my fresh clothes with care—my blue jeans, my clean red shirt, my white high-tops with the black check mark.

I caught a glimpse of myself in the glass tiles. I hadn't been talking to my reflection like I had when I first arrived; instead, I'd talk to Grandpa Archie. But on this morning I felt *fresh*. "Hey," I nodded at myself, "you look good."

At school, I whizzed down the slide and got back in line. I noticed a bit of dust on the toe of my shoe and cleaned it off. A kid came up to me and pointed toward my feet. I puffed up, fully expecting a compliment about my kicks.

"What you got on, fool? Some fake Nikes."

"What do you mean Nikes? What's Nike?"

I didn't know what Nike was, but I did know that this kid meant to shame me. My face got hot.

"Man, those are Kmart shoes!"

Steel rippled through my back.

"Whatchu talking about?"

"You got fake Jordache on too." He laughed.

My hands flew up. I shoved him hard. He pushed me back. Suddenly Ms. Smith was standing over us, and she sent me to the principal's office. I missed recess, but it didn't stop me from fighting.

I fought when someone was mean to me. I fought when someone told me I couldn't do something. I also fought to learn. Reading was a struggle for me. Even though I'd gone to school a little bit back in Sandtown, I hadn't really been taught. But in first grade at Cross Country, I was expected to read, and that was a fight. When I got tired of fighting with the words, Grandma was there to push me. She sat beside me at the kitchen table every day, helping me sound out each letter until the gobbledygook became words, and the words became sentences, and the sentences became stories. I had to repeat first grade, but I learned to read.

7

The Kool-Aid Test

My second year in first grade, I walked myself to school. I had a metal Incredible Hulk lunchbox and Grandma always made sure there were two sandwiches in it—one I ate on the way to school, no matter how much oatmeal I'd eaten that morning, and one I ate at lunch.

I was obsessed with the Incredible Hulk. Grandpa Archie and Granddad and I would sit in the basement watching the show together. My friends and I would re-create Incredible Hulk stories on the playground at recess.

Dontae Winslow lived nearby. He was real small and real smart.

I took my inspiration from Hulk: We smash stuff. We just pick it up and we break it. He took his inspiration from Spider-Man. "Naw, man, Spider-Man. Spider-Man is, like, sophisticated."

"Spider-Man is what?"

We would go to Luckman Park, down the block from the McClains' house, and wrestle. I especially liked to play with the McCoy brothers because they let us body-slam them. We would dig for worms and climb the wall between the tennis and basketball courts until we heard the song of the ice cream truck, and then we'd rampage out of the park.

Granddad drove the Number 5 bus, but he had a side hustle selling frozen cups, which was just frozen Kool-Aid. I was pretty much allowed to have those always, but I had to pay for them. They were twenty-five cents each, so if I ate three of them I owed him seventy-five cents, and never once did he say, don't worry about it. He'd take a big pitcher and fill white Styrofoam cups. In the giant freezer in the basement there'd be a layer of grape cups with a piece of cardboard on top, a layer of fruit punch with a piece of cardboard on top, and then whatever other flavors he had—watermelon or strawberry lemonade. He kept a few of the popular ones in the kitchen freezer, and in the pantry there was a cup with change. So people would knock on our back door and ask for whatever flavor they craved.

"Can I get a frozen cup?" asked a sweaty teenager with his arm draped lazily over a basketball.

"Today we got grape, strawberry, and orange."

"Give me an orange."

I put his quarter in the change cup and pulled an orange cup out of the freezer. Everyone at Luckman Park came to our house for frozen cups.

But what I really craved was a creamy orange Push-Up from the ice cream truck. Just like I knew where Grandpa Archie kept his peppermints, I knew where he kept his wallet and I'd help myself to ice cream money. Grandpa never said a thing.

Dontae and I sat on the curb trying to stop the heat from melting our treats before we could lick every last bit of cold sweetness from them.

"You want to come back to my house?" Dontae asked as he chewed the flat, pale bottom of the wafer cone. A trickle of orange cream ran down my chin.

"I better go home. My mom is going to be coming over soon." My stomach fluttered as I said it. She'd call every now and then, but I hadn't seen her in months. She'd tried to come see me, but something had come up each time.

Mama had called the week before and asked Grandma if she could come for dinner. Vivian, brow furrowed and lips pursed, handed me the phone.

"Hi, Mama. You gonna come soon?"

"Yes, baby. I'm gonna come next week and I'm gonna bring you something special."

I grinned from ear to ear.

I cleaned the orange stick off my fingers and scrubbed my face. I straightened up my room to make sure there was space for Mama to stay, if she wanted to. I waited. I took out the trash when Vivian asked me to. I waited. I went out to the porch. I waited. Mama didn't come. While I waited, I overheard Grandma quietly say to Granddad, "We cannot keep doing this."

I didn't cry. I didn't ask why Mama wasn't coming. I just went to find Grandpa Archie, who was watching an Orioles game in his room. I sat close to him listening to "Macho Duck" and holding peppermints on my tongue until they dissolved.

Mama didn't come that day. Or the next week. Or the week after that. But she did come eventually.

Ding-dong. I raced to the door and flung it open. Mama swung me up and I wrapped my limbs around her and buried my face in her neck. She said my name over and over again. When she set me down Grandma was standing behind us.

"Hi, Vivian."

"Hello, Tinka. Glad you made it this time!" Grandma called my mom by her childhood nickname.

Mama and I walked up to my room, my head nestled into her waist, leaving Grandma at the bottom of the stairs. We sat on the bed and talked for a long while. I just wanted her to stay with me at Grandma and Granddad's forever.

"Baby, it's going to be different from now on. I'm gettin' my life together. I'm gonna get a job and a place of my own."

We talked about what it would be like if we had a house.

"You would have your own room, with a door," she promised.

Mama hung out with Angie and Rhonda and Robert. We all sat out back at the picnic table near the watermelon patch and vegetable garden, and they would tell me stories about coming to see me in the hospital when I was born and being able to fit me in their hands. They'd talk about Grandma Maude, Vivian's mom and Grandpa Archie's wife. She made cakes and was always feeding the entire neighborhood. They'd talk about how tough Vivian was to please. She was the warden and they couldn't wait to get out of that house. "Man, she's so mean. How's she gonna have guests over and we gotta clean the house. We've got to wash every damn cup in this house." They started giving me advice on how to avoid trouble with Grandma.

"Boy, when she tell you to do something, just do it because she ain't going to shut up."

Angie repeated the advice Grandpa had given me. "Look, when she tell you to take the trash out, don't say okay, I'll do it later. Just do it when she tells you, okay?"

I nodded.

Then Uncle Ricky started telling me how to go about sneaking the snacks I craved. "Look, man, if you go and eat the cookies, make sure you do it when she is not in the house," he told me. "We can hear you open the box all the way up in the attic."

I was not sneaky.

On one occasion Grandma definitely knew someone had taken the cookies and she wanted the thief to fess up. "I know one of ya'll ate the damn cookies, those cookies ain't just get off the stove and walk out the house. Somebody ate the cookies!" Everyone looked at me. *What kind of cookie is going to walk out of the house?* I wondered.

I had a real sweet tooth—ice cream, peppermints, cookies, and Kool-Aid. The sweet tang. The bright color. Grape Kool-Aid was my favorite. It is an amazing substance. Granddad made Kool-Aid; my Grandma made sugar—when she made a pitcher of Kool-Aid it made your teeth hurt. After one cup of Kool-Aid, I wasn't allowed to have more unless I asked, and the answer wasn't always yes. I'd creep into the kitchen with ninja stealth and pour a cup anyway, but Grandma or Granddad would always catch me.

"When you get the Kool-Aid," Uncle Ricky advised, "make sure you don't use the same cup you were using. You were using that cup earlier for water, right?"

"Yeah," I said, though I had no idea where he was going.

"Then you went and got some Kool-Aid in that cup, right?" he asked.

"Yeah. I don't know how she knew I got the Kool-Aid."

"You left the cup on the table and there wasn't water in it, there was the red from the fruit punch."

"Damn."

The next day I put his advice to the test. "Granddad, can I have a glass of Kool-Aid?"

"No, Ricky. Wait till after dinner."

Mama watched Granddad leave the kitchen. She pulled me in to her. "Ricky, go get the Kool-Aid and bring it up to our room. If Dad asks, tell him it's for me."

I opened the fridge, stood on the stool that I used for washing dishes, and poured a tall glass of cool, red tropical punch.

Granddad walked in as the liquid sloshed to the top of the glass. "Boy, who's that Kool-Aid for?"

"It's for my mom," I said easily, and left him in the kitchen. But I wasn't slick.

I walked up the steps concentrating hard on not spilling a drop. When I was a few steps up, I just stopped and gulped the Kool-Aid down.

"What you doing?" Granddad's voice was sharp. "I thought the Kool-Aid was for your mom. You gonna lie about this?"

Every muscle in my body tensed.

Busted.

Mama came down the stairs.

"Dad, he ain't lying, it was for me."

"Then why that *mama temper* drinking it?" Granddad never cussed. He'd say *you mama temper*, or *you bunch of mud suckers*, or *what the helmet is going on in this house?* But I never heard him swear. "I said no and that means no. You don't like it, buy your own. As long as you live under this roof, you gonna obey."

Grandma walked into the hallway and stood there shaking her head at the pair of us. "Mmmmm hmmmm. Don't make no sense."

Mama and I slunk upstairs and sat in my room, whispering. "Why you ain't look back?" she asked me.

"I don't know."

"You ain't think he was gonna watch you? You shoulda waited till you got up here."

The next morning Granddad made breakfast and Grandma asked me to wipe up the table. Mama and I got to talking and I didn't wipe up. That was enough to launch Grandma into a sermon. "I told you to wipe up the table. You know, I wish all I had to do was just live with someone and wash the kitchen table and get every meal and have rent paid for and have a roof over my head. Lord, I tell you, it just don't make no sense. Lord have mercy. I tell you . . . Cheryl, did I ask you to take out the trash? Man, nobody don't do nothing around this house but me. I'm the only one who does stuff around this house."

Mama stiffened beside me, but she held her tongue. She just took out the trash and went upstairs. When I found her in our room, she had put on the white ruffled shirt with the little ribbon flower, and she was putting her stuff in a trash bag.

When she saw me, she said, "I love you, but I can't do this."

My heart fell into my throat. I wanted her to stay, but Mama and Grandma clashed. Mama wanted her freedom—on the street she just lived her way. But with Grandma there were a lot of rules and they had better be followed—hers was a traditional Southern Baptist church household.

I trailed Mama as she went down the stairs and into the kitchen and announced, "I'm leaving." Everyone was quiet. "But I'll be back."

"Uh-huh," Grandma grunted.

"I said I'll be back."

"Okay."

I followed her to the door and she hugged me goodbye, holding me for a long time. She smelled of baby powder. I loved her. She was still my mom. But I didn't even think about leaving with her. I was already home.

Other goodbyes were much harder.

When I was nine years old, I perched beside Grandpa Archie on his bed. There was a baseball game on. The Orioles were playing the Toronto Blue Jays, and they were winning.

Grandpa turned to me. "I want you to wash me up and make sure that I'm clean."

I was working at dissolving a peppermint without chewing it.

"Okay, Grandpa."

But before I could get him to the bathroom, Grandma came in and told me to get ready to go to Aunt Margie's house. Margie was the mother of Angie's boyfriend—I went to her house all the time. She was kind and caring and a fierce Uno player. We were slamming the black and white cards onto the table when the phone rang. Margie said a few words into the receiver, twisting the long curly cord around her finger. Then she handed me the phone. It was Grandma.

"Your Grandpa Archie died."

I began to cry big, ugly sobs. I cried so hard I couldn't swallow. Snot ran over my lip and I could taste the salt.

Margie's daughter said, "People die all the time."

"But he was my friend. You don't understand, my grandpa died."

Angie brought me home and Grandma and Granddad held me. I went to Grandpa's room and sat on the edge of the bed, as if he were still lying in it. I stared at the dark TV screen and kept hearing his voice when he had asked me to wash him up real good. Every time I thought of him asking me to wash him, my chest would heave and a new wave of sobs would break over me.

Grandma came in and tried to get me to come out. I wouldn't budge. Granddad came in. I stayed rooted to the bed. My eyes glazed over as I stared relentlessly at the flowers on the comforter. Then Robert came in and said, "Grandpa is thinking about you. He went the way he wanted to. Just so you know, I washed him up real good."

He patted me on the back and walked across the hall to talk to Grandma and Granddad. Robert was supposed to get Grandpa Archie's room, but he told Vivian and Richard that I should have it.

I just stayed in that room, as close as I could get to Grandpa.

8

Trumpet Lessons

By the time we were in fourth grade, Dontae was the skateboarding, avant-garde dude with thick-soled skate shoes and gloves, and he wore his hair in an s-curl. I didn't care much about clothes—if I had on pants and a buttoned-up shirt, and I didn't stink too bad, I was good.

That year we had to choose between taking PE or band. It was an easy choice for me; I was always the last one picked for anything athletic, and I was always getting injured. When Dontae and I walked into the band room, it was filled with students and clarinets, flutes, trumpets, and oboes, and there was a line of people with shiny brass instruments.

A man who played the trombone demonstrated each instrument, telling us a little about them and that we should think about what we wanted to play.

I leaned in toward Dontae. "Yo, we should play the trumpet. It's only got three valves. It can't be that hard."

That was it—we picked the trumpet.

At first, it was just something to do, and I enjoyed it a lot more than regular schoolwork. We rented Bundy instruments. We practiced. Then band became a place where I belonged. Everyone was a little different, but we were all different together. Band nerds, band geeks, whatever you want to call us. Suddenly, I was part of a group. I didn't want to miss school because I had band.

Dontae and I would walk together or meet outside every morning for eight o'clock practice. Gotta be at school at eight—band. Band. Band. Walking home, I practiced how to buzz. Lips too tight. Lips too loose. My whole mouth filled with the vibration. The hard trumpet case wiggled from side to side, knocking against my leg so that I stumbled home buzzing, like a drunk bumblebee.

On Christmas morning when I dashed downstairs picking the sleep out of my eyes, I saw a sea of gifts spilling out from under the tree. Granddad and I had gone out and chopped down the tree a couple of weekends before, then we'd brought it home and the whole family had decorated it with lights, ornaments, and shiny angel hair that dripped off every branch.

Half the living room was filled with gifts for me, and sitting atop the sea was a black case. I looked at Grandma and Granddad and smiled ear to ear. I popped open the latches and the trumpet glowed within its nest of red felt. The fabric was smooth and soft to the touch. I even had my own mouthpiece! I put it to my lips and buzzed.

Grandma cooked a giant breakfast—grits and fried salmon cakes— and Granddad put on old family movies on a reel-to-reel machine. An image of me as a baby, small as a bug on my first Christmas, flickered on the screen. There were old films of my mom too, and all my aunts and uncles as they grew up, opening presents up under a tree in this room with much younger versions of Grandma and Granddad.

I'd never really had discipline before. The discipline of doing. Coming home and getting my homework done was a foreign concept to me. When I got home from school, sometimes Angie would be there and sometimes Grandma, who would be cooking dinner.

She would ask, "Did you do your homework?"

"I think so. Yes." But I rarely did. I didn't care if I made good grades.

I'd rather be out at the park playing. Or down at the basketball courts with Craig Bowie, Brandon McCray, Anthony Bell, and Ronald Higgs.

So it wasn't shocking to me when, at parent-teacher conferences, Ms. Novak, my fourth-grade teacher, would sit across from Grandma and Granddad and say, "Richard is not doing his homework. In fact, he's doing nothing."

Physically, I towered above my classmates, but my reading and math were terrible, and whenever I got a test back there'd be red Xs all down the side. I'd slip the paper in the trash bin and not think about it. Ms. Novak (who was also a martial arts expert) didn't feel as nonchalant as I did. In the spring, she called Grandma in for a meeting with the principal and her tone was much more dire.

Ms. Novak sat across from me and Grandma, who leaned forward in the small student chair, looking even more imposing and powerful than usual. The principal was sitting with her back straight when she spoke. "We probably should fail him, but he's so big, we don't really want to do that."

Grandma nodded and said she understood. Then she marched me out of Ms. Novak's room. I kept my eyes on the brick floor as we moved down the hallway, its green-tiled walls closing in tight. Outside, I got into the red Pinto without saying a word.

When she broke the silence, it was a litany of punishments. "No more video games, no phone, no nothing. You're going to get this together or you're going to be the biggest dummy in the fourth grade."

When she said that, I didn't argue. I didn't say anything, but I sat up straight and thought, *You don't call me no dummy. I ain't no dummy. I'm going to make you say I'm smart.*

"I don't know what we're going to do, but we're taking all these things away from you and we're hoping for the best."

Granddad came home from work. He was thin and stood high above me, and the blue shirt and charcoal pants of his bus driver uniform made him look even taller. After Grandma gave him the rundown he thought for a minute, then slowly said, "Well, he likes that trumpet, so let's take it away."

While Granddad marched up to my room, Grandma said, "You can do when you want to do, you just don't want to. Uh-huh. We gonna take this trumpet and see."

Granddad clomped back down. "If you want this trumpet back, you have to do better in school."

I stomped up to my room. *You take my trumpet, I'll show you. I'll fix you. I'll get my trumpet back.* I knew I'd do whatever it took. I was determined not to screw up. The trumpet had all the answers. I had to get it back.

I started doing my homework for the first time and my work was paying off. In language arts we had a test about contractions. I knew just where to break the word, what letter to drop, and where the apostrophe went. I wrote down all the answers and the next day when Ms. Novak handed me my paper, there was a sticker and a smiley face looking back at me. I had got 100 percent.

"Wonderful work, Richard. You *can* do it." She beamed. I floated on her praise. It was a raft that carried me away from failing. I wasn't the biggest dummy in fourth grade.

When my grades started turning Grandma didn't shower me with affection or pride, she simply said, "Uh-huh, that's what I said. When you want to do, you can do." But there was no mistaking the joy in her eyes as she said it.

9

Band Nerd

"What's that?" I pointed at the sousaphone Corey was playing. "I want to play that." Nothing else in the band room looked like it. Nothing else sounded like it.

When Dontae and I got to Fallstaff Middle School we were still playing trumpets, but I was trumpet eighteen out of twenty-eight. When Mr. Burns, the band director, opened the big metal door to the giant instrument vault, I saw that instrument—the big curve of its bell, its three valves wrapped in beautiful circuitry, and its singularity. It was the only one I wanted.

Mr. Burns smiled at my scrawny little self. I was pretty tall, but still whip thin. "Well, how about you move to baritone horn first?" So I played baritone for a little while, and then at the end of seventh grade I moved to the sousaphone. By then, I was the only sousaphone player, but that had some disadvantages.

Beside the green chalkboard was the Musical Star Chart—a grid with gold stars and colorful badges. For every pop song you mastered, you got a star. The wall was filled with stars earned by the flutists and trumpeters for being able to play the theme song to *Sanford and Son* or *The Cosby Show*.

I wanted to play Stevie Wonder's "I Just Called to Say I Love You" so badly. I asked Mr. Burns about the music for sousaphone.

"No one has ever requested this, so I don't have an arrangement for sousaphone."

"Oh, so I can't play any stars?" I looked at him with the biggest, saddest puppy-dog eyes.

So Mr. Burns arranged all the popular tunes for the sousaphone.

He would teach us by rote. He would play whatever I was learning on the piano and then I would try to play it back. He'd play, *Dee Deee Di*.

I'd play, *Dee Dee Dooooo*.

He'd say, "No."

We'd do it again and again until I played *Dee Deee Di*, just right.

When I wasn't working with Mr. Burns, I would be in a tiny soundproof box of a practice room with a cassette tape.

I'd press Play and a voice would say, "This is B-flat. *Doooo*. Pause the tape. When you have mastered B-flat, go to C."

Then I would play *Do-Re, Do-Me, Do-Fa, Do-Sol*, until I could hit each note again and again.

I was the first sousaphone player to get all the stars on the board.

But I was not getting any stars in my academic classes. Nor was I getting good marks for behavior. I was always being called into the principal's office. For fights. For grades. For attitude. That big brown bench facing the secretary's desk practically had my butt imprinted on it; I sat on it more than I sat in class. Social studies with Ms. Jackson had way too many cute girls to impress.

One day Grandma arrived and we went in together.

Ms. Shaw, the vice principal, eyed me, and then she looked at Grandma. "Richard has . . ."

I broke in, "But I'm not . . ."

"Excuse me. I'm talking," Ms. Shaw said sharply.

Then quick as can be, I flipped, "Excuse me, *I'm* talking." Heart pounding.

Ms. Shaw's jaw flapped open, but no sound came out.

Grandma roared, "EXCUUUUUUSE me. You must have lost your

damn mind. I will come up to this school and whip your ass in front of the whole class if you don't change your attitude."

I stayed quiet. I knew she wasn't bluffing. Anger was bubbling out of her, her voice was tight and loud, and then all of a sudden she was crying.

"Me and your grandpa are trying our best. We're giving you all we can. We really need you to change." She was fishing in her purse for a tissue.

Ms. Shaw held out a box of Kleenex.

"Lord, I don't know what else to do." Grandma was rocking back and forth. "Lord have mercy."

We left the office and I studied the ground, occasionally glancing up at Grandma, but her brow was still knitted together and I knew this was a storm that wouldn't pass.

My feet dragged. I was afraid to be too close to her. I'd been hurt plenty, but I don't think I'd hurt anyone that way before. I was ashamed. These people had never given up on me, but now, maybe they'd send me back to Mama.

I slid into the front seat of the red Pinto and stayed quiet.

I was on fire. I burned with shame—not that I'd done poorly in school, but that I had pushed Grandma beyond tears, beyond exhaustion, to the point where she was at her wit's end.

When Granddad got home from work that night Grandma unloaded: "I was gonna kill him. Richard, I was gonna kill him! I've never been so embarrassed in my life. What are we gonna do? Lord. Lord. Lord."

The next day when I walked into the kitchen all Grandma said to me was, "Ricky, you can do when you want to do, you just don't want to." Then she handed me an epic list of chores and left for work.

I got up the next day and did the chores before she woke up. As I wiped down the mopboard, I thought, *Okay. Now what are you gonna tell me to do?*

When she came downstairs later that morning I said, "I've taken out the trash, wiped down the trash can, put the dishes in the drying rack, swept the floors, and wiped down the mopboard."

There must have been hubris in my tone because she swiftly said, "Well, then why don't you clean the dishes in the china cabinet and wipe down the shelves."

Her list of housework was endless.

To my chores, I added my homework.

The worst punishment was that I had to drop out of band until my grades improved. I was stuck in typing down the hall, tortured by the sound of music echoing off the classroom walls of the band room as I tried to hunt and peck beneath the hard plastic baskets we had to place over the keyboards and our hands to keep us from hunting and pecking. My wrists chafed against the rough edges. The only thing I got from typing was motivation to get out of typing, which is not to say that I learned how to type. I sucked at typing. I was so terrible that I was going to fail, so they let me back into band.

I learned music by ear. I couldn't read sheet music but I could play "I Just Called to Say I Love You" and an aria from Mozart's *The Magic Flute*. That's how I got into TWIGS—To Work in Gaining Skills—the junior program that was a sort of training ground for kids who wanted to get to Baltimore School for the Arts. Dontae, our friends Sandra and Maria, and I all auditioned for the free after-school arts program when they came recruiting at Fallstaff. Sandra got in for dance, Maria for theater, and Dontae for trumpet. We thought we were the kids from *Fame*.

The band kids were my tribe. But with the TWIGS program, I was out of my element. The kids in TWIGS had been playing instruments for a lot longer than I had, they had private lessons, they could read sheet music, they owned their instruments. There weren't a whole lot of brown kids running around TWIGS. It was Dontae, Sandra, Maria, me, and a whole bunch of white kids from different parts of the city.

My instructor was Ed Goldstein. We would meet at the Baltimore School for the Arts in a practice room on the fifth floor. Ed gave me assignments. He told me I had to get this book, Getchell's *First Book of Practical Studies for Tuba*. Granddad and I didn't even know where to get the book, so we drove all the way to Silver Spring, Maryland, to find it. Up to that point, I'd never practiced outside school. I didn't know you were supposed to sit down and spend hours trying to learn the music. I didn't have a recording of the music we were playing. I didn't know how it was supposed to sound. I didn't know I was supposed to be able to read music. I looked at those rows of black dots and saw ribbons of gibberish.

I could sense Ed's frustration. I'd play and he'd say, "No. Do it again." Round and round we went. I knew I wasn't getting it, but I didn't understand why or how to fix it. Everyone else understood it and I didn't. How do you look at these obscure dots on the page and know what they mean? I wanted to be able to do that. Everything was new to me, but I was determined to grow great. I did not understand the meaning of the word "quit."

Once I got serious about sousaphone, Mr. Burns, the band director, would put the big white instrument in the back of his gold 1986 Honda Accord and take me home so I could practice over the weekend. Then, he'd pick me up Monday morning to bring me back to school. The instrument didn't have a hard case, so we had to take it apart. We put the bell in first, and then the body of the sousaphone would have to be placed over the bell, so it would all fit in the trunk.

At school I had this crazy sousaphone chair—part seat, part instrument-holding contraption with three spidery prongs to support the body of my instrument. I was still a pretty scrawny kid and couldn't hold the sousaphone and play it unsupported. But at home I didn't have a sousaphone chair so I practiced a little bit at a time until my shoulder couldn't take any more. I'd try to balance it on the chair in Grandpa Archie's old room, then I'd crawl up under the sousaphone, shimmy up into its tubes, and play. That's where Grandma found me practicing. I wanted to finish before Mama showed up for dinner.

The last time she had called, she had promised to bring me something.

"What is it?" I'd asked.

"Something," she said, her voice full of mystery.

"What is it, Ma? What are you gonna bring me? Is it cars? Is it a truck?"

"I promise, I'm gonna bring you something."

My imagination took off running. Maybe she's going to bring a race car, or a spaceship. My mind went crazy. I asked Grandma what she thought it was. She just shrugged.

"Your mom is on the phone, Baby Ricky." Her tone was clipped and I knew before I'd picked up the receiver that Mama wasn't coming.

She explained that she didn't have the bus fare. All I could do was mumble that I understood.

As I slipped back into my room, I could hear Grandma say, "You just don't see him. You can't keep doing this to the boy."

I was torn. I loved my mom but I was old enough to understand that Grandma was right. I needed someone to take care of me.

I raised the sousaphone up and let my fingers fly over the valves. I played *Do Do Doooooo Do Do Doooooo* until my lips were numb and my fingers started to cramp.

By the end of seventh grade, I was the kid who played sousaphone. Or tuba, as all the nonband kids called it. Or the bugle, as my Granddad and the people in my neighborhood called it. Sousaphone. Tuba. Bugle. Whatever. I loved it.

It felt like something I could do that belonged to me. Something I could do that very few people could. Of course, it helped that I picked an instrument that no one else had wanted to play. It was a way for me to communicate with something that I understood on a really comforting level. It didn't have to be explained in any complicated manner and I could do it as many times as it took to get it right. Playing music was like a light going on in the dark. Like seeing a star for the first time.

10

Cracking

"Yo, you got a watermelon head and a tiny body. Why your head so big?" Michael cracked, as Dontae and I walked from the band room past the gym. The group of boys standing behind him snickered.

We kept walking.

"Look at the band nerds. Time to make the music," one of the other boys said in a sing-song voice.

"Leave it," Dontae told me under his breath.

"Band is stupid," Michael needled again.

I spun on my heels and yelled, "Band is not stupid, you don't know what you're talking about!"

"You shut up. I'll punch you in your mouth."

"No. I'll punch you in the mouth. Wait till after school."

As I walked around for the rest of the day, I could hear the other kids chattering, *After school they're gonna fight. Where they gonna fight? On the playground.*

At the sound of the last bell, I swung my book bag over my shoulder and slammed my locker shut. Sandra was staring me down. "Richie, don't fight him. It's not worth it."

"He said band is stupid."

"He's an idiot."

But I didn't know how to back down. I headed out to the grassy scrap of lawn behind the low brick building.

Outside, Michael was waiting. I tossed my backpack on the ground and got in the enemy's face. We were as close as we could be without touching. I could feel his hot, stanky breath on mine.

I kept thinking, *Just don't touch me. You better not touch me. If you touch me, it is on. If you touch me, I'm gonna knock you out.* My whole body was a live wire.

Kids gathered around, willing us to fight. Dontae and Sandra were on the sidelines with some of the band kids.

"Yo, he said your mother was stupid," someone egged me on. I saw Michael smirk and I rushed him.

I leaned all my weight and all my anger into him. He stumbled, then grabbed me. We grappled. I caught him off balance and seized him. He threw a punch. I hit the ground hard. It felt like my lungs had been shut in a box. I sucked air but there was no oxygen.

I staggered up, but as soon as I was on my feet, he planted his meaty hands on my shoulders and shoved me hard. I fell again.

"The tuba is stupid," he spat at me, each word a sledgehammer.

I heard the sound of fabric ripping and saw a big patch of my knee peeking out through a hole in my pants.

Mr. Marshall strode out from the portable classroom, a fierce look on his face. In a flash he pulled Michael off me and sent us to the office.

When I walked in the door that afternoon, Grandma took one look at the rip in my pants and asked, "What happened?"

"I fell."

"What do you mean you fell?"

"I fell."

"How'd you get the hole in your pants?"

"I just fell."

"What do you mean? You just walked outside and you fell?"

"Yes, ma'am."

"All right. Well, since you don't know how you fell or you *just* fell, we're going to put a patch on them. You gonna wear these pants." She sewed on a big country patch and I wore them to school.

"Aaaah, you gotta patch on your pants." One of Michael's friends laughed and pointed.

I stepped up to him. "I'll see you after school."

The Saturday after Grandma had patched my pants, the chore list was infinite. She'd left it on my bed while I was still sleeping. I'd read it lying in bed and rolled my eyes. But there was nothing to do but start. The house was quiet when I began making my bed, until I heard the chorus of my boys.

"Yo! Richard!"

"Come on, man."

"Yo, we're going to the basketball court. Ya'll got some frozen cups in there?"

Chris Hall, Craig Bowie, Ronald Higgs, Brandon McCray, Anthony Bell, and me had been running around the neighborhood together since I'd arrived at the McClains'.

Grandma and Granddad were deeply faithful people. They went to this giant Baptist church, Gillis Memorial on Park Heights Avenue. I went there a few times with them, but once I made friends with Craig, Ronald, Anthony, Brandon, and Chris, I started going to St. John's United Methodist down the street. We'd walk to church together, or Chris's grandfather Mr. Orange would give us a ride (he taught us Sunday school), or Craig's mother, Ms. Laura, would pick me up and I'd go with his family. Four of us had a quartet and we would sing with the boys' choir. We'd walk to Sunday school singing, "This little light of mine / I'm gonna let it shine," and "Oh, when the saints / go marching in," and talking about how we'd be famous singers one day.

They used to call for me through the window, and I'd always tell them I'd come out when my chores were done, but the work would take me hours, and sometimes by the time I got outside, they were heading home. One day Craig said, "Yo, let us help you." So they started coming over on Saturdays and together we worked through my chore list and then headed out to the courts.

"Let me see the list, yo," Craig said as he walked through the front door.

Make sure the dishes are washed, dried, and put away.
Clean the baseboards in the house.
Make sure you rake and bag the leaves.
Make sure you mop the basement floor.
Clean the china in the china cabinet and dust the cabinet shelves.

The way I knew I was in big trouble was when she wrote, *Make sure you clean the windows.*

Oh man. I hated those windows. They were old-school windows with a crank at the bottom that you turned to open and shut the slats of glass. The entire kitchen was filled with these. You couldn't just take a rag and clean the whole window, you had to unscrew the braces, take the screen out, and then wipe down each rectangle of glass.

"Hey, Baby Rick." Ronald giggled. "Why you always washing the dishes? Yo, every time I walk down the street I see your lil' head sticking out, yo."

Anthony laughed but asked, "Yo, where's the bucket? Yo, where's the mop? I got the basement floor, yo."

"Yo, where are the rags?" Craig asked. "I got the windows."

"All right then, yo."

Chores done, we'd all head to the Luckman Park courts to play basketball. I needn't have bothered. Aside from football, I sucked at sports. I'm the guy who, when teams were being picked and there were only two people left, would look over at whoever was beside me and think, *Awww shit, I guess ya'll are going to pick him.* I was that kid.

We played ball and hung out. There'd be a couple cars at the top of the street playing music, a hub of people by the water fountain, a family playing tennis. Then someone would come through singing out his sales pitch: "Yo, I got that blue, I got that hot blue. It's fire, yo. It's fire," as if he were selling cold soda or hot dogs.

I was leaning against a fence talking to Craig when I felt the energy at the courts shift. Suddenly, Carl appeared. He was a couple years older than me and glided across the court, one ripple of muscle. He was the boss and if he showed up, that meant there was a problem and shit had to be rectified.

Everything got quiet. Time slowed down. Heads nodded as Carl came toward me. "Yo, you get outta here, shorty," he said in his Southern accent. He was looking at me. When he spoke, everyone paid attention. Everybody on the court was watching me. I didn't say anything. I didn't move either.

"I told you to get outta here."

"Whatchu yelling at me for?"

"Get out of here," Carl insisted.

"Ain't no one else getting out."

"You got that bugle thing going for you. You gonna be somebody. Go home."

"But . . ."

"Yo, take him home now." Carl gestured to another boy on the court.

I didn't pay his compliment any mind, but Carl was the boss of the court. He had street cred and his words carried weight.

The boy he'd gestured to came over. "Yo, let's go get some freeze cups." Everyone knew my granddad sold the Kool-Aid frozen cups from our back door. So this dude, Craig, Ronald, Chris, and I traipsed back to my place and sat on the front porch sucking at the frozen cups and turning the block of ice upside down to get the sugar that pooled at the bottom. Our tongues and lips stained red, purple, and orange, we disappeared inside to play video games. Granddad and Grandma always made sure I had the latest video system so that I wouldn't be out getting in trouble on the streets.

Although I was never picked on the basketball court, the football field was a different story. I *could* play football and I loved it. I played nose guard and center. I was going to be a football player and make a million bucks by the time I was thirty. All I had to do was keep a 75 percent average so I could go to Carver Vocational-Technical High School, play football, and train to be a carpenter just in case the football thing didn't work out. As much as I loved playing in band, that wasn't something I could make a living doing and my grades weren't good enough to get me into a school with a great band program—at least not one with a football program too. I had my eyes on the prize.

"I'm going to go to school for arts," Dontae told me. "You should audition too."

"Yo, that's wack. Whatchu going to go to that school for?"

Dontae didn't pay my foolishness any mind. He knew what he wanted and he loved that trumpet more than anything.

I played for a recreational football team, CC Jackson on Park Heights Avenue. By eighth grade I was too big to play with the ten-to-twelve-year-olds, so they had me playing with the fourteen- and fifteen-year-olds. I was playing football with the big boys. Most of the time, coach never put me in because I was so small. I got tired of sitting on the sidelines and decided not to show up to a game—and then we had to forfeit because we didn't have enough players. *Oops.*

The other boys on the team were from Park Heights. They were men to me. I was scared, but they were always supportive, calling out, "You got this," or "Come on. You got to step it up," and "You can't quit, shorty."

Pickup games were a whole other league though. One day Craig and Ronald and I were headed to Pimlico field. We walked through the neighborhood, gathering a flock of boys who wanted to play.

"Yo, where are ya'll going?" Anthony called from his porch.

"We're about to go play football."

"Oh, let me go get my shoes."

Suddenly our little group had grown to six, eight, fourteen kids. On the field we joined the grown men and divided up into two teams.

I was running the ball. We'd get three yards and they kept getting the ball to me and we kept getting more yards.

I was talking smack. "Yo, you can't stop me. Ya'll don't know. I can do this all day. All day." I ran my mouth relentlessly and watched them get frustrated. "Yo, you're grown men and you can't even stop me."

The barb landed and two guys strode up to me and without saying a word they each picked up a leg and pulled in opposite directions. A third man pushed me over the top so that I flipped, landing hard on my back.

I lay on the grass looking up at the sky. Something was wrong. There was an electrical fire shooting from my hip to my heart, which jumped with adrenaline every time I tried to move. I dragged myself up onto my feet, but pain exploded and rolled over my body and I fell back to the ground.

I was telling my leg to move and it would not.

I heard one of the older boys say, "Daaaaaammmn. That's what you get for running your mouth."

"Stop playing, Richard," Ronald said.

"I ain't playing, man. Help me."

My friends crowded around me and heaved me up. "Come on. Walk," Craig said. They half carried, half dragged me to the edge of the grassy field.

"I can't, man. I can't."

"Shake it off, man. You tough," Craig urged.

"I really can't."

A storm was pushing in on dark clouds and then the air was filled with rain. Everyone scattered and Craig said, "I'm gonna go get your granddad, yo." Then he was gone too. Anthony stayed with me.

I lay in the soft grass, under the dark clouds, being pelted by cold rain.

When I was three, a year or so before I moved in with Richard and Vivian, I was roaming the streets at dusk. I'd been out playing all day and the other kids had gone home for supper. I kicked at a pebble on the sidewalk and tried to ignore the rumble in my stomach. But all

I wanted was food: Chicken wings. Cheese. Cookies. Potato chips. Salt. Crunch.

I passed a building with a light on in the basement. On a little plastic table was a bag of chips, shiny and bright and unopened. I waited. No one came back. The two basement windows were just my height. I tucked into the corner next to the stoop and peeked in one more time.

I drove my sneaker into the glass. Smash. Crack. Shatter. The window exploded.

My foot dangled off my leg. Blood ran out and formed small rivers on the sidewalk.

I was real quiet. Everything was real quiet and far away.

A couple rushed over and wrapped my foot up in a kitchen towel. Mama appeared. Someone poured a bottle of peroxide over my ankle and white bubbles and blood erupted onto the sidewalk.

"Cheryl, I'll go call an ambulance," the woman who wrapped up my ankle said.

"Naw. I'll carry him to the hospital." Mama scooped me up and held me close to her. "You gonna be all right, baby." My blood was soaking the towel.

The hospital was not close. She moved me from her arms to her back.

"Mama, maybe we should call an ambulance."

"We can't afford no ambulance. I got you. It's gonna be fine."

At the hospital, Mama rushed through the doors. Everything was giant and cold. Suddenly there were lots of hands on me. They put me on a gurney and rushed me into the ER. The doctor was a man. A nurse gave me one shot after another, trying to numb my leg. I screamed until my throat felt raw. I couldn't feel pain, but I watched the needle dive in and out of my skin and felt the tug as they pulled the thread taut. I squeezed my eyes shut tight.

When I left the hospital, they measured me for crutches. The next day, my cousin Tracey and I had turned them into swords.

By the time Granddad found me on the field, I was wetter than a shark in the ocean. "Boy, they got you good."

Anthony and Craig helped Granddad get me off the field into the back seat of his yellow Lincoln Continental.

At home, Grandma fussed over me and dumped a carton of Epsom salts into a hot bath. She never liked me playing football.

The next morning when I hobbled into the kitchen, each step sent a hot wire into my brain. Grandma took one look at my face and said, "We're going to Mercy."

She was the shipping and receiving supervisor at Mercy Medical Center. When the doctor saw me, he told me my hip was sprained, that it would heal on its own, and that in the meantime I should use crutches, which I did for two months.

I crutched through the halls of Fallstaff and swung myself along sidewalks back and forth to school. I balanced my crutches on my sousaphone chair during band practice. Then I dumped my crutches and got a cane.

I got so tired of it. I was done with the cane, and I threw it aside like James Brown shedding his cape, but instead of leaping up and walking, all I could do was wobble. It hurt like hell. I had an awkward limp, somewhere between walking and dancing.

My friends called me Gimp.

"This ain't right. You can't walk straight," Grandma said, and took me back to Mercy. This time I saw the doctor who had done Grandma's knee replacement and he immediately ordered X-rays. It turned out my hip was dislocated.

He told us that they could put two metal pins in my hip. When I asked him about playing football, he said, "This is serious. If you get hit the wrong way, you won't walk again."

Then he handed my crutches back to me.

11

Saturday School

"Granddad! I'm going to go audition for School for the Arts."

"When?"

"Now. Let's go."

"What, it's today?" He didn't know any better.

"Yeah."

"We're going right now?"

"Yeah. Now."

"Okay, where's the bugle?" he asked, referring to my sousaphone, which I had already taken apart and set near the door to the garage—the body, the bell, the mouthpiece.

"I've got it."

"All right, let's go."

My brain hadn't stopped spinning since I left the doctor's office. I couldn't play football, but I really didn't want to be a carpenter. That had been my backup plan. The only other thing I had going for me was this instrument.

On Cathedral Street, Granddad pulled up in front of the copper awning over the doors to Baltimore School for the Arts. He hopped out, set the sousaphone down near the door, and drove off to find parking.

I fit the pieces of my white fiberglass sousaphone together. I was ready. The first door I tried was locked. It was Saturday. The school was dark and quiet. I hoisted the sousaphone up on my shoulder and crutched my way along the line of doors until I found one that was open.

I'd come here for TWIGS a hundred times, but today it was different. There were no students and the entrance hall expanded out above me. It was a cathedral—all light and air and high, high ceilings and an elegant spiral staircase that swept up to rooms where music and art and dance happened. I imagined walking up those stairs every day.

A man with wire-rimmed glasses and blond hair asked, "Can I help you?"

"Yeah. I'm here to audition."

"Excuse me? The auditions were yesterday."

"But I'm here today."

He didn't say anything. I didn't say anything either.

Finally, he led me into an elevator and walked me to a practice room with a piano and a music stand.

"Please play the piece you prepared."

I played a bass aria from *The Magic Flute*.

"Okay." Then he set out some music that he wanted me to sight-read. "Can you read this?"

"No."

He cocked an eyebrow at me. "But you can read this?" And he pointed to the aria I had just played.

"Yeah."

He pointed to the sight reading and asked, "Do you know what this is?"

"Yeah. This." I pressed down the first valve.

"But do you know what note that is?"

"Yeah." I played it again.

"That's B-flat," he told me. "Hmmmmm. You have no idea how this goes?" Then he went to the piano. "Can you play this?"

He ran his fingers over the keys. *Do La Sol Fa Mi Re Do.* I played it back to him.

"Wow." He sat at the piano for a moment. "Hmmm. Okay, I'll be right back."

When he came back he said, "You must be one of the luckiest young men on the planet. I talked to some of the faculty and we are going to accept you into the Baltimore School for the Arts."

"Okay," I said, and walked out like he'd just told me we were having meatloaf for dinner.

When I hobbled outside, Grandad was there waiting.

"I'm done," I said.

"All right."

"I got in," I told him as he drove off.

"Okay, good."

When we got home I called Dontae from the phone in the kitchen. "Yo, I got into Baltimore School for the Arts. *We* going to School for the Arts."

"Yo, that's crazy. We went to Cross Country, Fallstaff, and now School for the Arts together!" We both started laughing.

Then he paused. "I ain't seen you at the auditions."

"I auditioned today."

"What? But the auditions already happened."

I explained how everything went down. "You lyin'!"

Part II

CHANCE. CHOICE. CHANGE!

The second time the New Mexico Symphony Orchestra held auditions, I saw the listing in the American Federation of Musicians journal and was surprised. Brock Campbell, the tubist who had won the position after my first audition, hadn't gotten tenure. So I sent my résumé in and was again invited.

I had worked hard. I felt great about my playing. I was ready to win a principal tuba chair. But I couldn't afford to go. Auditions easily cost more than a thousand dollars a pop and I had already maxed out my student loans paying for room and board and lesson fees, buying a tuba I could be competitive on, and going to auditions from Denver to Rochester to Savannah.

Mr. P—Daniel Perantoni, the tuba professor at Indiana University Jacobs School of Music—was sure I was on the verge of getting a job. "You're going to the New Mexico audition?" he asked.

"No. I can't."

"What do you mean you can't? You're ready. You sound better than ever, Rich."

"I can't afford it."

"Don't worry about how much. You go find the plane ticket. I got it." My chest tightened. "Thank you."

"But Rich, let's be quiet about it."

Yet again, I was being offered a chance.

I went. I played. I played better than I had the last time I was in Albuquerque. I did not advance beyond the first round.

Orchestral auditions are like the Olympics: You can give it all you got and still come up short. I gave it all I had at the time, but I still wasn't on the level.

There was a click in my brain, like a tiny gate opening, and in crept doubt. *What's happening here? What am I doing? Man, I can't even get out of the first round.*

I needed something to hold on to, something to keep me going. But all I had was myself. I had to bring more. I had to bring my absolute best—thorough, detailed, complete. I had to change.

12

Flip the Script

Freshman year. I had my boom box with large double D batteries. Run-DMC. Forum Adidas shoes that I used all my allowance to buy in every color. Russell sweatpants, which always matched my shoes. White on white. Royal blue on white. Black on white.

I showed up at Baltimore School for the Arts. I was a Yo Boy.

Students pushed through the big front doors in waves and the principal, Dr. Simons, greeted each and every one of us. That day, I had on a crisp pair of sweatpants and my fresh white shoes. Dr. Simons stopped me and said, "You know we have a dress code here. We don't wear sweatpants to school. This is the first day. This is your warning." The dress code was pretty simple, a shirt and no sweatpants, but I wasn't abiding by it.

"Okay," I said, and marched into the school.

The school had been an old hotel. There was a spiral staircase and Greek pillars in the lobby, the concert hall was the old banquet hall complete with a chandelier, and when we had assembly, they'd roll out the bleachers that had curtains draped down the back. The classrooms were small—they were old hotel rooms and our classes never had more than twenty or twenty-five people.

When the hour struck, the hallways filled with people. I stood with

Dontae near the gray metal lockers, light flooding in from the windows. The visual art students had colorful hair and loud clothes, the theater players *were* loud, the musicians had instruments on their backs, and the vocalists were singing. But everyone was walking to their next class. There was no teacher patrolling.

"There ain't no bells here? We just go to class?" I stared at all of them, like bees moving through a hive.

"Yup," Dontae said.

"We can just walk out the front door and leave?"

"Yeah, and you can come back in too. So you can go out and eat lunch."

I brought my lunch every day. The idea that someone would buy their lunch was decadent and exotic.

"Oh, wow. What kind of place is this?" The question hung between us.

"Yo, this is what the white people do. They go out for lunch."

The next morning, I put on a fresh pair of sweatpants. Dr. Simons pulled me aside. "Come here, Mr. White. You want to know the difference between the Baltimore School for the Arts and the rest of the schools?"

"Yes, sir."

In a very soft and very clear voice he told me, "At this school the adults run the school, not the students. You will go home and you will change your clothes and you will adhere to the dress code, or you will not be in this school."

I skulked home, changed my clothes, and came back.

I ain't no punk though, I can't just do what the white people are tellin' me to do. I was convinced the school was trying to make me white. The next day I slipped into a pair of sweats, but I put a pair of jeans in my book bag.

When Dontae saw me on the way to school he said, "Yo, you're still going to wear those pants?"

"Yo, I wear what I want to wear."

We walked into school and Dr. Simons stopped me. "You know you can't wear that, go home and change. Now."

"Okay." I changed into the jeans in my bag.

When Dontae saw me later that morning, he called me out. "Yo, there ain't no way you could gone home that quick, yo. You must have brought the clothes."

"I ain't bring no clothes, man."

"You had to. How else you gonna explain it?"

I admitted to his observation. "Yeah, I put the jeans in my book bag."

"That's stupid, yo. Just wear the jeans."

After that I wore jeans. Besides, no one here cared about my sweats or my shoes. Everyone was busy doing what he or she had come here to do.

Dr. Simons changed the way I dressed and the other teachers went to work on the way I spoke. I was corrected whenever I said that someone *axed* instead of *asked*. There's nothing *strong* with that when I was trying to say there's nothing *wrong* with that. And if I used *ain't*, I was pushed to rephrase what I was saying. It was exhausting.

I complained about the school trying to change me to a skinny up-perclassman with a raspy voice named Tupac Shakur, who schooled me. "It's deeper than that, man. It is a reflection of yourself, yo, you got to represent." I stared at my lunch, which I'd set out on the long gray cafeteria table. I just nodded, not really knowing what he was talking about.

Tupac was a nerd with a nose ring. No muscles. No tattoos. He had nappy hair and wore Oxford shirts with buttons on the collar, so the flaps wouldn't fly up. But when he spoke, I listened.

He thought for a moment and then said, "It's like the Black Panthers. What do you know about the Black Panthers?" I didn't know his mother was a Black Panther. I didn't really know what Black Power was.

"Nothing." I shifted on the bench.

"Come on, man, you gotta read. You don't read enough, man. You have to know your history. We got to create change, brother. People create opportunities for us, man, you've got to take advantage." My brain was spinning. *Are you on the white people's side? Are you on my side?* He was way above my head. He was the dude who could perform Shakespeare *and* give daily Black Panther sermons in the basement, and at the end of them, he'd bust a rap. He was Black Lives Matter before Black Lives Matter.

Tupac told me, "We want a fighting chance. We want the same thing they want. You put one hundred people in a shoebox and see how that works out. That's what the projects are." I learned from him about Malcolm X, when I'd been raised on MLK. I had never met someone who was so street and so articulate. He could speak better than some of the teachers, and could relate and communicate on a higher level.

My brain was overloaded. I didn't know what to do with half of what he was telling me. But when he started talking through music, I could hear everything.

We had a group, Rap and Tap. Tupac and James Parker, the other tubist at School for the Arts, rapped. David Cole Quick would tap dance. I would rap a little, beatbox, and play a rhythm on the long cafeteria table.

My first freestyle at BSFA flowed out of me:

Yes, I'm livin' on a messed-up planet! Cause on the news
The freakin' media so confused
They got the public thinking I'm ignorant 'cause
I'm writing funky lyrics never listening to my verse
All they hearing is my cursin'
But the words that I'm sayin'
Coming straight from my brain to the street
Niggas pumping up my sound cause they like to hear my beat!
RAW most definitely. I am hardcore
I bust a rhyme and leave you wanting more.

Tupac had a fat medical records notebook where he'd dash down ideas. "You always have to be ready. You don't know when inspiration is going to come," he would say, bopping his nappy head up and down as he wrote a new rhyme. He also carried a big black three-ring binder full of raps. He'd flip it open during lunch and we would just jam right there. He perched on the edge of the table and directed.

He pointed at James. "You go, 'What's up—what's up—what's up.'" James was short, with a chipped tooth and all the confidence of a star. He was a Yo Boy like me, but whereas I had one foot in the hood and one foot out, he was still firmly rooted there.

"You go 'Boom. Boom. Boom.'" Tupac looked at me with his big eyes and nodded. He hit the table, building a bass thump. He'd conduct—pointing and banging and beatboxing until we had the rhythm going, and then he'd open his notebook and start to spit.

A group of kids walked over from the Ping-Pong table, and others left their lunches and stood around us listening, bouncing their heads, clapping, joining in. We were all caught in the spell. Even there, at a cafeteria table, the music Tupac created made us lean toward greatness.

I'd never gone to school with so many different types of kids. But they tended to hang out with the students who looked like them—the Jewish kids stuck together, as did the kids, mostly white, who got bused in from Annapolis, where the Naval Academy and the State House of Representatives are. Those kids wore their privilege like a uniform you could button up and use to gain passage to a whole other world. One that was shiny and safe and in which they belonged. Then there were the kids from the inner city who stuck together, who were Black and brown. There was a sense among us that we were not supposed to date across race lines. We had solidarity, but there was also still room for differences, which was something I had to get comfortable with.

I didn't know how to handle lots of things. Another upperclassman, Jada Pinkett, hung out with all the dancers and I marveled at how all the young women and men touched each other. Some of those boys would touch the girls' butts and it would be nothing. If one of us had done it, we would have had our head knocked off.

Jada was hanging on Kelly, Roger, and Skia, and suddenly I was rocked by the idea that she didn't draw lines between girls and boys. I put all my ignorance on full display. "Ewww, you like girls."

"This is why I can't stand immature, big-headed freshmen. I wish they would get rid of all of them."

"I ain't going nowhere." I may not have been leaving, but I still had a lot to learn. I wanted to be respected, but first I had to earn it.

When I arrived at Baltimore School for the Arts, I graduated from the sousaphone to the tuba.

James and I were the only two tubists in the school and the music department had a closet full of tubas. There were so many that I could keep one at home and one in my big wooden instrument locker at school. In the closet were two brand-new upright piston B-flat Yamaha tubas, big, beautiful instruments with the valves perched on top, but I didn't know how to hold them. I was used to my sousaphone, with its special spidery chair. Holding the tuba was difficult. I had to learn how to support it with my legs, and to find the right height I had to spread my thighs to lower the instrument or push them together to lift it up.

James had been playing the tuba, but because he was so small he couldn't hold it properly, he just played the Yamaha sideways. He was first tuba, which meant I sat to the left of him, and he'd hold his tuba on its side and his sound would just blow right through my ear.

Chris Ford would say, "James, can you please hold the tuba correctly?"

James wouldn't budge. He just kept on blowing me away with his sound.

It didn't matter how James held the tuba, he could play the hell out of it—he could play piano a little bit too. When I looked at the Yamaha crooked in his arms, I clung to the thought, *Well, you can play better than me, but I can at least hold it properly.*

When I walked into applied lessons, my old TWIGS instructor Ed Goldstein greeted me. "So you made it."

In middle school, I'd loved playing in band, but TWIGS wasn't fun—it was serious. And from the beginning, Ed labeled me as lazy.

One afternoon after I got out of school at Fallstaff, Granddad dropped me off for my lesson. Ed had told me to learn the Getchell études. Études are musical exercises designed to practice and improve the fundamental skills.

"You play in your band. You're the star of your middle school. I know that you can play. I know that you *can* do this, but that you're just not working hard enough. You really need to practice." His pale eyes peered at me through wire-framed glasses. I couldn't look him in the eye so I stared at the shiny spot on the top of his head. "Play measure one and two," he instructed.

I played.

"Now, do it again."

I did.

"Now, say the rhythm."

I did.

"That took thirty seconds. How much better are you?"

I wanted to scream, *You have no idea how hard this is.* But I didn't say anything. I didn't tell him that I didn't have lessons, or that I had never heard the music we were playing, or that I couldn't read music.

I bluffed my way through TWIGS.

Ed would sit in front of me and say, "For next week, I want you to play Getchell's one through ten." Then he'd pick up his instrument and play *Do Re, Do Mi, Do Fa . . . Be, Bee, Beee, Beeee.*

I heard the first few measures and the next week I played them back by ear, but I'd butcher the rest of the song. Hacking away at notes and rhythms I could only guess at.

But after my audition for Baltimore School for the Arts, Chris Ford had explained to Ed that I couldn't read sheet music, so Ed started working with me. We had proficiency tests, and I learned to read music enough to get by. I was also learning about music in choir and brass ensemble. Ms. Foulkes taught this class and was the first person to introduce me to rhythm cards—flash cards with rhythmic notations that can be rearranged for the students to clap and say the rhythm.

I still wasn't pushing myself.

In my applied lesson, Ed and I sat facing each other in the practice room. *Boooh.* I played the last note. I knew it was bad, and not bad meaning good either. I figured Ed would tell me, "Richard, this is unacceptable. Why didn't you practice?" I wouldn't say much and then we'd both go on our way.

Instead Ed looked at me for a good, long while.

"You know how much I actually get paid to be here?"

I shrugged. *Don't know. Don't care. Where's this going?* I fixed my eyes on the red walls and the foam soundproofing.

Ed walked away and sat in the windowsill, the sun bright behind him.

"I make thirty dollars an hour to come teach you every week. By the time I drive here, pay for parking, I'm probably making ten or fifteen bucks to teach you. Do you think I need that? I don't have to do this." His voice quavered.

"I work to support my wife and family. I do this because . . ." He stopped talking.

I ground my feet into the carpet.

"I don't know what I'm going to do . . ." His voice trailed off. There was nothing left for him to say to me.

"I'm sorry," I said quietly.

He raised his shoulders in surrender, then said, "It's up to you."

I started practicing, but I had no idea what was truly required.

As I left school for the day, Dr. Simons asked, "How're you doing today, Richard?"

"All right."

"Did you have a good day? Did you practice?"

"Yeah, I practiced a whole half hour today. I'm on fire," I boasted.

"A whole half hour, really? How long did that take you?"

"Huh? Thirty minutes. Bye. See ya tomorrow."

Dontae was waiting for me on the sidewalk. We headed for the subway and I told him about the conversation with Dr. Simons.

"You lying." He busted up laughing. When he caught his breath he asked, "You went to Dr. Simons and bragged about practicing a whole half hour, yo?"

"Yeah. I think he liked it."

"Fool. A half hour is nothing."

"Well, how much you practice?" I asked Dontae.

"Yo, my warm-up is probably a half hour."

"Your what? What do you gotta warm up for?"

"Don't you warm up?"

"Naw."

"Well, what do you do every day?"

"I pick the tuba up and play it. Why do you gotta warm up?"

"I gotta get my high notes."

"I just play my high notes."

"I play my scales. I do my lip slurs. I got my whole routine."

"You do that and then you practice? What about the music we gotta play for choir?"

"Yeah, I do that after I warm up."

"Well, how long that take you?"

"About two hours a day."

"What?!"

I was floored.

"Is that how you've been getting A's on all the scales and the assignments?"

"Yeah, how you been doing it?"

The truth was that a half hour before our brass chamber music class tests, I'd ask someone what scale we were supposed to play. I'd talk them into playing it again so I could hear it, and then I'd practice it for a few minutes before Ms. Foulkes called us into the room.

"I kinda work on it before the test," I admitted, and Dontae started laughing his behind off. "That's why you be failin', dummy. Yo, everybody else practices all week."

"For real?"

"Yeah, man. We get the assignment on Monday, I look at it for the first time on Monday night. I'll figure it out Tuesday, then I practice it Wednesday, then I have a pretend test on Thursday, and then on Friday when the test comes, I already did it."

I stopped walking and looked Dontae in the eye. "Are you serious?"

He was dead serious. He was the smartest, realest person I knew.

One day after school, he took me to the Enoch Pratt Free Library. The building was enormous and white, and when I walked up those steps, I felt small. I had never been to a library before. It was quiet and clean and bright. The librarian smiled at us.

In a sunny atrium, Dontae flipped through card catalogs, calling out questions to me.

"What do you know about Mr. Harvey Phillips?"

"Nothing. Who cares?"

"He's the Paganini of tuba, yo."

I didn't say anything.

"What do you know about the Canadian Brass?"

"Nothing. Who cares?"

"It's the best brass quintet in the world."

I leafed through the sheet music they had and found the first tuba concerto ever written. The Vaughan Williams tuba concerto premiered in 1954. I brought it home.

13

Pool Party

I spent the summer after my freshman year getting ahead on the études. I took every music book that I had and tried to learn ten to fifteen études so that in September when Ed assigned me the études, I was far ahead of the game. But I was still behind.

There were ten of us in brass ensemble, and we sat in a small semi-circle and played in front of each other. Ms. Foulkes drilled us on scales and études. She was fierce, old-school, *and* hard-core. The previous year I scraped by, but I hadn't really been trying. Now, I actually practiced every day at school, and at night I would go over the assignments, but I still wasn't working hard enough.

"Dontae," Ms. Foulkes called.

Dontae stood, lifted his trumpet, and played the assigned scale, A major, so that I felt happy and sad and lifted in just a few moments.

"A," Ms. Foulkes said, and wrote the grade in her green book.

"Yeah," said Jennifer, a junior French horn player.

Everyone else smiled and nodded their heads. Then Ms. Foulkes called on me.

My stomach fluttered.

I sat up straight and told myself to just breathe in and play. I faltered at the scale and missed a few accidentals.

Ms. Foulkes listened and shook her head. "C. So, Richard, on the first assignment you got a C minus, on the second you got a D, on the third you got an F. You're in trouble. You're looking at a D in the class. We've got four or five more classes, so you have to get a B each week if you expect to pass."

I stared at the floor and felt everyone's eyes on me.

She bent over her grade book. Then she called on James.

He swung his tuba up into his arms. There was talent dripping off him. He coasted through the scale, set down his tuba, and leaned back satisfied, a smirk curling his lips. When it came to playing, James was downright cocky. He knew he was talented.

He didn't hang on Ms. Foulkes's words the way the rest of us did.

"A," Ms. Foulkes said. "You've had an A, a B plus, a B plus, and an A, and I don't see any problems here."

Class ended and everyone filed out of the room. I was still packing up when Jennifer walked up to me, her French horn hanging at her side. "Yo, why do you let him beat you all the time?"

"I don't know." I shrugged.

"Why don't you just practice? He shouldn't beat you. You're such a nice person I feel bad every time you get an F."

"You *could* get A's on the scales. You could be better than him if you just practiced and studied," Ms. Foulkes chimed in from behind us.

I nearly dropped my tuba.

Ms. Foulkes continued: "You know, you really shouldn't let him kick your butt."

The look on her face was flint and it struck against the steel in me and sparked.

That afternoon during my free period I went to an empty practice room and played the assigned scale until my lips were sore and numb, like I'd been kissing someone for an hour.

In early fall Ms. Foulkes announced that there would be auditions for the Greater Baltimore Youth Orchestra (GBYO).

Everyone encouraged me. They told me I had to practice, made sure I knew which études to study, and offered to come listen to me.

Jennifer sat with me in the practice room while I worked on an étude in 6/8. I was having a hard time with the rhythm and she said, "You've just got to feel it. You're going one, two, three, four five, six. You don't really count 6/8, you have to feel it."

"What are you talking about, feel it? If I don't count it, I ain't going to be able to play it."

We did it over and over until the music started to flow. I started to understand that the primary beats were one and two. A lock clicked open. I stopped thinking so much and the music came to me, filling every molecule of me until there was nowhere left, and then it poured out of my tuba. Jennifer smiled.

I had no intention of winning, but everyone was so supportive I wanted to give it my best shot. There'd be tuba players from all the other Baltimore schools auditioning, and James Parker was going to audition too. James could pick up the étude and read it straight-away. He could play it easily, beautifully. He made playing tuba look effortless.

I practiced my butt off. I started getting to school even earlier to practice. It didn't open until eight in the morning, but at seven thirty Sunny the janitor would open the door for me and say, "You hungry, man," approval in his voice as he ushered me into the building.

I'd take the elevator from the lobby up to the fifth floor and walk along the quiet hall to my locker, where I kept my tuba and all my schoolbooks. The locker was so big I could have ducked inside it.

I breathed in the silence and then filled the early morning quiet with a low roll of the tuba.

The day of the audition, Anne Harrigan, the conductor of the youth orchestra, came to our school and judged each of us.

I clearly hadn't been on her radar and when I finished, I saw a look of surprise on her face. "Wow, well done. We already have one tubist in

GBYO but we are going to take another. The audition results will be sent to your school."

A few weeks later Ms. Foulkes announced the results to us in class. I wanted to win. I worked hard, but I knew she was going to call James's name. Just the way I knew when he finished playing an assignment that she would say "A," almost automatically.

"For tuba they selected Richard."

The room broke into whoops. Everyone was grinning. I sat there, unable to speak. Ms. Foulkes walked up to me, said, "Congratulations, Richard," and gave me an elbow and a big white-person wink.

"Thank you, Ms. Foulkes," I whispered, as if saying it out loud might break the spell.

"You worked hard for this," Ms. Foulkes said.

There was a music board in the hall where they hung an announcement congratulating all the students who made GBYO, and there was my name: Richard Antoine White.

Everyone was surprised and there were rumbles all around school. *Richard beat James! How'd he do that?*

When I saw James he said, "Yeah. I really didn't practice so it's cool."

I overheard him explain to someone, "Well, I sight-read and Richard practiced a lot."

That was true. I had worked hard. I knew that there were people who were more talented than me, but I had learned that I could outwork anyone.

I navigated school like I had navigated the streets. Except for music, I did just enough to get by. School was not hard. It was just a matter of how much I was going to put into it and what the value of that work was to me. If there was a workaround, I found it.

In English class we were explicitly told not to read the CliffsNotes, but I did anyway.

When Mr. Grose asked me a question, I could discuss all the salient parts of the book and then soak in the praise. "Oh, wow. Great job read-ing, Richard. You got all the important parts." I nodded and thought, *Mr. Grose, you must have read the CliffsNotes too.*

The other kids got mad. We got an assignment back and Dontae looked over my shoulder. "Yo, what? You got a hundred? I read the whole book, man, and I got an eighty-eight."

"Yo, all the answers are in the CliffsNotes."

"Grose told us not to read the CliffsNotes."

"Every single answer is in the CliffsNotes, man."

"Yo, that ain't fair."

"Hey, you can get the CliffsNotes too."

He was not happy.

Most times he would get A's and I would chug along with a C, but that could leave him unhappy too.

In math, the teacher handed back our tests. I leaned onto the arm-rest of my fiberglass desk and asked Dontae, "What you get, man?"

"I got a hundred. What you get?"

"I got a seventy-two. But guess what, when you graduate and I grad-uate and we both cross the stage, our diplomas are going to say the same thing."

Dontae's face clouded over. He looked at me like I had stolen his life savings, and then he said, "You're right." From that moment on he worked a little less hard at the academics and devoted more time to his trumpet. But still, he was a more diligent student than I was.

One day, we were walking into English class when I admitted that I hadn't read Bram Stoker's *Dracula.*

"Don't worry about it, I got you," Dontae said, and gave me a dap.

This time, I hadn't even read the CliffsNotes, so when Mr. Grose asked who would like to share their thoughts on the book, I sank a little lower in my chair, but Dontae spoke up. "Richard would like to, Mr. Grose."

I cut my eyes at him.

Mr. Grose took one look at my face and said in a booming voice, "Richard, you didn't read . . . Out!"

Dontae held a fist to his mouth to stifle his snickering, but he couldn't keep quiet. "Dontae, you get out too," Mr. Grose said, and we slid our books off our desks.

"Serves you right," I said when we were out in the hall, and we both doubled over laughing.

Outside of tuba, I wasn't just resistant to doing the homework, I resisted authority. I may not have been trying to wear my sweatpants any longer, but I still managed to stir things up.

I was running off at the mouth in Ms. Gladney's English class. She was telling us how important a good thesis was and I argued, "It doesn't matter. If they understand you, then you get your point across. If you understand what I'm saying, why does it matter how I say it? I did not write all these fancy words you were telling me to write, but you understood my point, yes?" That was the wrong thing to say.

She was furious. "I will give you a zero if you do not shut up."

"Zero?" I said, incredulous.

"You get zero."

"Well, I . . ."

"Zero."

"I didn't . . ."

"You are not getting it, are you? Zero."

"That's what you get," Yazzy said. Yazzy was short for Yasmeen. We'd been friends since freshman year and she had a little crush on me. I could always count on her to give me the homework and a side hug if I hadn't finished it myself.

"He ain't going to shut up. He's so stupid," I heard a boy in the seat next to me say.

"You stupid. Don't call me stupid," I snapped.

As the words flew out of my mouth, Ms. Gladney announced, "Zero."

"But . . . ," I protested again.

"Zero. I'm talking. What part of 'shut up' did you not understand?"

I was mad. My eyes stung, but I held back the tears. I shut up, but I still had a lot to say.

"See me after class," Ms. Gladney said, and then moved on.

When I approached her desk, she opened her notebook to where she'd scrawled a string of zeros in line with my name.

"Do you think you deserve all these zeros?"

"No," I said, defiance sharpening my voice.

"Well, what was my instruction to you?"

I looked down at the ground. "To be quiet."

"Did you do it?"

All I could do was answer, "No."

"Do you think I was unfair now, based on you following my instructions?"

"You were fair," I muttered.

"Now what are you going to do about it?" she asked.

"Well, you gave me twenty-five zeros. I'm not coming to class."

"You are just going to give up that easy?" She stared at me hard and when I didn't say anything, she pressed: "If you put the same amount of energy into working as you did into telling me stuff, you could probably turn this around."

"How?"

I did extra book reports for Ms. Gladney till the end of the semester, but that didn't really change my attitude, though my writing did get better. Sometimes I'd skip class and head down to the practice rooms. If the rooms were taken, I'd sit on a bench in the hallway and play. The tuba music rolled through the halls, so that my teachers always knew where I was, even if I wasn't where I was meant to be. When I practiced, it was just me and the tuba. There wasn't anyone else telling me where I had to be or what I had to do. I was free.

I was fed up with everyone telling me that I could do more. I didn't want to do more. I just wanted to play.

Everyone knew that I loved the tuba and the teachers grew accustomed to hearing me practicing during class. They wouldn't let me cut corners and I always had to make up any work that I had missed, but they knew I wasn't skipping school or jerking around. I had come here to study tuba and I was working hard at that.

Tuba saved me, and not just existentially. Getting to school was an odyssey that began at 6:00 a.m. I'd take the Number 44 bus from Luckman Park to Rogers Avenue Station, walk upstairs to the train and ride it to State Center, catch another bus, and then walk to school. When rehearsal ended at 4:10 p.m., I'd turn around. The groups of kids scared me. I was jumped several times. I always stayed near the center of the platform, terrified that someone would jump me and I'd be thrown down onto the tracks.

One day a group of six or seven boys hopped on the train car and came up to where I was sitting, with my tuba resting between my legs. I was pretty sure they were going to kick my ass, and I thought, *Well, I'm gonna get one.* I scanned the group. *I'm gonna knock the tall skinny one straight out.*

"Oh, where you go?" one of the shorter kids said, staring down his nose at me.

"I go to Baltimore School for the Arts."

"Oh, you think you better than everyone else."

I looked at the boys. I thought about my tuba and I thought maybe I'd try to talk my way out of it. "Look, we should all get along, it doesn't matter what school we went to. . . ."

"Shut the hell up," the shorter kid spat at me.

This talking shit was some bullshit, but I couldn't fight, all I could think was that I had to protect the school's tuba. The tall kid I thought I could take swung at me, his fist landing on my cheek. I slipped off the seat and curled around the tuba.

Someone's foot slammed into my back, but I didn't let go of the instrument.

Then the train slowed and one of the boys, realizing I wasn't going to fight back, said, "Forget it." They slipped off the train. My tuba had saved me.

Sore and tired, I limped home, tuba in tow.

It wasn't just the kids who bothered me. All the homeless people made me sad. There were so many people perched on the street or walking along the platforms at the stations asking folks for money.

Dontae and I often traveled together. Once we passed a homeless man and he quietly said, "That's my dad."

"Yo, are you serious?"

"Yeah, man."

"Damn."

There were homeless people everywhere—at the stations and on the trains, and just a short walk from school, you could find them milling around Lexington Market. I'd read under the chandeliers at the Enoch Pratt Free Library and pass homeless people as I walked by the fancy law offices and the courthouse. If I could see these people, I knew that the politicians could see them too, and they chose not to do anything. They chose to ignore them. That fueled my anger.

By the time I was in tenth grade, I was six-foot-two, taller than all my friends and most of my teachers. But Ms. Geidt was even taller than me. She taught American government. We had learned about the abandonment of the gold standard and were studying the creation of the Federal Reserve. I resented it all—the rich representing the few and the rest of us being left behind. She was up there talking about an elegant system of checks and balances, but the system she described did not reflect my life, or the lives I saw every day.

I was angry. On top of all the suffering I saw and the indifference to it, I was sure the whole system was fixed. "This is all jacked. The rich people control this country. All these checks and balances—it doesn't matter."

Ms. Geidt argued, "You have to understand the structure. You need to know how your government works."

It would have been a healthy debate, except for my colorful words.

"Why are you spending all your time teaching us this bullshit? This system is fixed. This country is bullshit. No one is going to defend me."

She kept on trying to teach the class; I kept interjecting with a snort or an "eeh" or a "ha."

Ms. Geidt asked me to leave, and later she and Mr. King, one of the deans, pulled me aside in the hallway. Mr. King was bald and always wore a sports coat. He pushed his glasses up the bridge of his nose and fixed me in his gaze as Ms. Geidt described how disrespectful I had been. Heat flashed through me.

I got in her face and spat out, "I'm not a child. I am an adult. You do not talk to me like a child."

Ms. Geidt held her face real still. "If this were anyone else right now, I'd be scared. You're better than this, Richard." Then she turned the corner and was gone.

The anger drained out of me and I was filled with regret. I had changed since my arrival at Baltimore School for the Arts. I wasn't trying to flaunt the rules and I wasn't the big-headed freshman Jada had dismissed. I had found something I loved and I was working hard to make something of it. I knew that Ms. Geidt recognized that change. I didn't want to let her down. She gave me respect and I didn't want to let go of being respected. It had changed me. Instead, I wanted to return that respect.

I cooled off and went to find her. "That was really disrespectful. I'm sorry." Our relationship changed. Ms. Geidt showed me that you can maintain your integrity and still keep it 100 percent real. She also handed me a shield. She taught me that if you are educated and aware of the law and your rights, you are better able to defend and equip yourself. Knowledge is the fiercest weapon you can have.

In the school basement, there was a Ping-Pong table and an Olympic-sized swimming pool, which we were expressly forbidden from going near unless we were in gym class. Being down there, we were in a world apart. There was big open space, a long stretch of windows that let in light from the street, and air that smelled of chlorine.

We congregated around the Ping-Pong tables—Yazzy, James, Keisha,

Roger, and a few other kids—playing doubles matches, talking smack, and killing time before the after-school rehearsals for *Les Misérables* began. Keisha was a theater major but always hung out with the musicians because she and Dontae were dating.

Time passed real slow that afternoon. Someone wandered off to explore. Someone got close to the pool. Someone dragged a hand across the water. James suggested dumping the cleaning machine into the pool. Keisha giggled. Yazzy laughed. Our cheers surfed across the water. Before I knew what had happened, someone had pushed the machine close to the edge. Our shouts echoed off the wide windows. Then, the machine was in the water. *Splash. Bloop. Blu. Blu. Blu.* It sank into the water and we dissolved into laughter. I couldn't catch my breath, I was laughing so hard, like when I was a kid and Ricky Jr. would tickle me to the point of tears, and I thought I might die if I didn't get some air in my lungs.

"Who did that?" one of us asked.

Boom.

"I was over here," Yazzy said.

"It wasn't me," I said.

"I didn't even touch it," someone else chimed in.

"Well, it didn't just fall in there," Keisha challenged.

"I think it did," I said, and giggled nervously. I didn't know who'd actually done it, but we'd all taken part. This was bad. My throat sank into my heart, my heart sank into my belly, my belly sank into my toes. All at once I was ill and empty and filled with dread.

We scattered.

Soon the group of us found ourselves sitting in the wooden chairs lining the waiting room outside the dean's office. No one spoke. Legs bounced, lips were chewed, cuticles were bitten back to the raw nubs. I wanted to use the restroom, bad, but was afraid to ask permission to walk down the hall.

We were each called in, one by one.

Every time Mr. King appeared, I thought about how I had let these people down after they had taken a chance on me. I didn't want to be a disappointment. I didn't want to be expelled.

Stephen, a singer who had been with us, was called into Mr. King's office first. When he emerged, he said, "I'm out." My stomach, which was now somewhere outside my body, tumbled and dove.

James and I exchanged a look.

Shame swooped in my gut. But then, I felt a blaze of anger. Yes, I had been part of the trouble, but I had spent the better part of the last two years changing my voice, my clothes, my everything, and now, when I had bought into what this school was selling, they were going to kick me out. Even though I'd been part of something dumb, the thought that they would kick me out after hijacking my identity set me on fire. *I did all this shit for you*, I thought. *After all the changes and challenges I faced each day just to get to school, these white people are going to shut the door on me.*

Keisha went in next, and when she came out of the office, she said, "I'm in."

Mr. King called James in. When he came out his shoulders were slumped and his voice was real low. "Yo, I got expelled."

I was sure I was done. This was going to be my last day at the School for the Arts.

Dr. Ford appeared behind James and looked me in the eye. "Richard."

The room was carpeted and quiet. Mr. King, Dr. Ford, and Mr. Moore, the academic dean, sat on one side of the long wooden conference table and I sat in the lone chair facing them.

"Richard," Mr. King said, his voice heavy with disappointment, "someone could've drowned today." Dread snaked through me. "You and your fellow students were destroying property in a place you were not supposed to be."

"Do you have anything to say for yourself?" Dr. Ford asked.

I could have been humble, I could have apologized. But the words that erupted out of my mouth had nothing to do with what happened at the pool, it was as if I had to defend the integrity of everyone who had ever felt under- or misrepresented. "This school is some bullshit. You guys are trying to make me white. You're always telling me how to talk. I can't wear my clothes. You don't really care about me, you just want me to be like you."

A long silence stretched over the room.

Finally, Mr. Moore asked, "That's what you really think?"

I looked at him real hard but didn't say anything else.

"We're actually trying to help you. This is the way most educated people speak. This is the way most professionals dress."

"Well, you were lucky because if there was another school for the arts, I wouldn't be here." I caught Dr. Ford's eye. The air went out of the room. It disappeared from my lungs. There was no space, no oxygen. I couldn't believe I'd said that.

The moment stretched and stretched. My heart sank into the pit of my stomach. I waited for yelling, for expulsion, for the full weight of all the power sitting across the table to come crashing down on me. Instead, Mr. King spoke very calmly. "Richard, being at this school is an opportunity and you should take advantage of that. For some reason everyone sees tremendous potential in you. How about we find out what it is they see?"

"Okay," I said, my mouth barely forming the word.

"Richard, what you did today was wrong, but we're not going to kick you out. We are going to put you on zero tolerance policy. If you even think wrong, you are out of here. If you mess around, your fate will be much the same as James's," Mr. Moore said.

Oxygen rushed back into the room. My lungs filled. My heart floated out of my stomach. I could breathe. I wanted to shout out my sweet relief, but I quietly thanked them and walked into the waiting room.

I nodded at Roger and Yazzy. "I'm in."

As I said those words, I understood that I was in control of my destiny—what happened next, whether I failed or succeeded, was entirely dependent on me.

14

Yo-Yo Ma Should Be Sad
He Plays the Cello

I sat down and played the étude. It felt good. I coasted along the bass notes and when I was done, I grinned at Ed and puffed myself up.

Before he could even get a word out, I was bragging. "I can even play the high notes." For weeks I had been trying to increase my range and it had finally happened.

Ed cocked an eyebrow.

"Yeah, that's good, and if you keep at it you could be a pretty good tuba player. But there are a lot of good tuba players and I don't know a single one who has been hired."

"What do you mean they're good?"

"To get hired, to play in an orchestra or a quintet and actually make a living, you have to be great. You have to be better than everyone else. Good isn't enough."

You could practically hear the air hissing out of me.

I wasn't going to play football. I wasn't a star student. I wasn't even learning carpentry. I had no backup. All I had was tuba.

I started getting to school at seven in the morning. Sunny would sometimes press a sandwich into my hands when he opened the door for me with what had become his morning greeting, "You hungry."

I was. I would not be a loser. I would not let anyone be better than me.

There was an open class in the Margaret Armstrong Recital Hall—that meant all the music students had to attend and the hall was full. I slipped into one of the black chairs. There was a man sitting center stage holding a tuba. He was soft and unassuming, with glasses, pale skin, and pale blond hair. I had no idea who he was, but when he played, I saw that he was a genius god.

The notes looped inside my skull and shuddered down my spine, setting off explosions of noise and light and joy and heartbreak.

Everyone else in the hall disappeared. The music coming from the tuba was everything. I had heard Ed play in the Peabody Ragtime Ensemble, but I had never heard tuba music like it was coming out of the bell of this man's instrument. It possessed a voice that could be magical and passionate and emotional.

Pride rushed through me. I didn't *just* play tuba, I played an instrument that could speak to anyone. *Man, Yo-Yo Ma should be sad he plays the cello.*

David Fedderly was the principal tubist for the Baltimore Symphony Orchestra. After he played, he talked about technique and breathing. I joined him onstage, heart thrumming, and played an étude for him.

He listened stone-faced. I was sweating. I'd never wanted to impress anyone the way I wanted to impress him.

When I finished, he raised his tuba to his lips and played the same étude. It sounded like an entirely different piece of music.

Fedderly corrected my posture, my breathing. "You're not playing this rhythm right. You need to count. Let's go." I couldn't count it. He stopped and said, "You've got a lot of work to do. But if you get it done, we will see what happens. There are a lot of problems there, but I think we can fix them."

He ripped me apart. But I had heard him play and I wanted to play

like that. I took in every word he said, embarrassment and desire ripping through me.

The first time I had played my trumpet in church, I was in fifth
grade. I performed "When the Saints Go Marching In." The church
had old red hymnals and wooden bench seats with one long red cushion
stretched across each row. When it was time for me to play, I sat right
next to the piano, alone. I started on a wrong note and kept going down
from there. That song was unrecognizable. But I kept blowing into that
horn until the end of the song. It was like someone had cut out the
lights on me—*Who cut out the lights? Where am I? What do I have in my
hand?* The sound coming out of my trumpet sounded like a whale song.
Everyone looked at me. But this was church. God was going to protect
me. Right?

"Man, you're not that good, huh?" Chris Hall observed when I was
done.

"You play all the time?" one boy whispered.

Marsha was the only friend I had in church that day. "You keep going, you'll get it."

My embarrassment hardened into determination and I worked
harder. Playing for Fedderly was like that. I knew I wasn't good enough,
but man, I wanted to be.

Fedderly's playing was like a drug. It permeated my brain. His tuba
became the sound in my head. I needed to hear him play again.

I got a job as an usher at the Baltimore Symphony's home, Joseph
Meyerhoff Symphony Hall.

The music I heard sounded just like the records I had started listening to at home. I would stand in the aisles, directing blue-haired white
ladies and their husbands to their seats, and then stand by the door
with my eyes glued on Fedderly. I noticed how he sat before he played.
I noticed when he played soft or loud, I watched how he breathed and
how he supported the orchestra—there's only one tuba player in the
orchestra and everyone relies on the tuba player for pitch and rhythm.

At the end of the concert, I'd help people out of the theater, then dash to the backstage door and wait for Fedderly to walk out. As soon as I saw him, I bombarded him with questions.

"Just come on back, Richard," Fedderly told me, and gave me the punch code so I could go backstage whenever I wanted. I felt like I had keys to the White House.

I opened the backstage door and saw mailboxes and cubicles—the space was gray and carpeted and totally forgettable. But then I turned the corner and saw a giant black bass instrument case standing against the wall. Hard cases littered the floor, lying on the floor or leaning against the rows of lockers—these were straight-up gym lockers—but instead of athletic shorts, there were tuxedos hanging inside each one. They looked shiny and dapper and I imagined putting one on.

Fedderly had already changed by the time I found him. I tripped over myself to ask him questions. "Oh my gosh, how did you do that? It was really loud here, and then it looked like you were asleep, and then you just came in."

He smiled and nodded his head. He answered all my questions and told me stories of studying under Arnold Jacobs at the Chicago Symphony Orchestra. And it wasn't just Fedderly. I went backstage all the time and talked to everyone—the violinists, the trombone players. The whole orchestra fanned out before me and I wanted nothing more than to be part of it.

Once, I walked onstage after a show, just to know what it was like. The whole house was quiet. The floor shone brightly and the waves of white box seats rolled toward me. I closed my eyes and imagined playing on that stage.

I had one manager at the Meyerhoff—let's call him Dream Killer Manager—who was a white dude with crew-cut hair, always wearing a J.Crew sweater with a collared shirt and khakis.

Dream Killer Manager spoke to me like I was a Negro kid he was helping out, a Negro kid who should feel very lucky that I had been given a job at the Meyerhoff.

"Be on time, Richard."

"Tuck your shirt in, Richard."

"Smile, Richard."

"Speak clearly, Richard."

Standing in the lobby with another usher and Dream Killer Manager one evening, a zing of recognition shot through me when I heard the opening notes to a piece I knew. "We played this at school!" It was Borodin's Polovtsian Dances.

Dream Killer Manager shrugged and said, "Yeah, sure," in a tone that left no doubt that the only thing he was sure of was that this Black boy standing in front of him could never play *that* music.

The other usher had beautiful fingernails that were always long and manicured and painted bright colors. She was tickled pink that I too had manicured nails that were trim and clean and painted with clear polish. I told her that I wanted to play for the symphony. She listened and was encouraging. "You'll be up there one day, honey." But Dream Killer Manager sneered: "You're never gonna be up there. That's where the big boys play."

My fist flexed but I held my tongue.

"You better not let me catch you opening that door to listen to the concert," he warned, and walked away.

He'd patrol the hall to make sure we weren't inside.

When he was out of earshot, I looked at the other usher. "I'm gonna play on that stage one day and he's going to bring me a bottle of water."

15

Any Given Day

"Mr. Grose, it is a tough world out here, man. Would you actually pun-ish me for something I didn't do?"

"What are you talking about, Richard? Absolutely not."

"Good, because I didn't do my homework."

The whole class laughed.

"Richard. Out," he said, stifling his laughter.

After class Dontae and I headed to the cafeteria. He took out a bag of potato chips.

We had borrowed money to get a couple bags of chips at Rite Aid the day before. Dontae just didn't have money, but I spent all the money I earned and my allowance on my girlfriend, Danielle. We went to school together. She was a really talented vocalist and cool and kind and beau-tiful. I'd pissed her off one day and to make up for it, I'd brought her a gift once a week. I never missed a week. The worst gift I ever gave her was a whole set of big grandma curlers. Her mom busted out laughing, the biggest belly laugh I'd ever heard.

I inhaled my bag in thirty seconds flat. But every bite Dontae took was a meditation, and after he'd eaten half the bag he neatly folded the top down.

"You still eating that bag of chips?"

"Yeah, man. I saved it."

I could connect the dots. Things were tight in his house. His mom had been real sick for years. She had been raped and was dying of AIDS. Each time I saw her she was smaller and smaller. I was scared as hell of AIDS, and I was scared as hell of her. Whenever I went to Dontae's grandma's house on North Avenue, I was afraid to use the forks or spoons; I was afraid I'd contract the virus. I was afraid of what I didn't know.

Riding the train together to the State Center subway stop by school, Dontae and I talked about girls, school, and our moms. He talked to me about his mom and his uncles who lived at his grandma's house on North Avenue and were drug dealers. I told him about my mom, her drinking, and moving around all the time.

I'd started out in Sandtown and then moved uptown—from the hood to the suburbs. But in elementary school, Dontae lived in the big, rich house right next to school, and then we got to Fallstaff and Dontae moved to North Avenue in the hood. Our lives seemed to be moving in opposite directions.

One day he mentioned going to Lafayette Market. Just the mention of the place made me feel small and brought the taste of those chicken gizzards rushing back.

"Yo, how you know that place?"

"That's where I used to live."

He didn't tell me that he was hungry, but I knew. Their refrigerator was always empty. Dontae's breakfast often consisted of egg sandwiches or the chicken wings we would get at the local store. We sat in choir at eight in the morning sucking those bones and then chucking them at the back of people's heads. We would also sit back there and fart. It was horrendous. Ms. Johnson, the voice teacher and assistant choir director, said, "All right, Richard, get it together, we don't need any sudden expulsions of air."

Everyone laughed, but the first time she said it, I asked Dontae, "What is she saying?"

"She's saying don't fart, yo," Dontae told me in a harsh whisper.

"Oh, farting is a sudden expulsion of air. Who says that?"

We ate. We farted. We sang. Dontae had that super bass. He could sing incredibly low. I sang like a broken whistle *and* I sang loud, like I was nailing it.

I was so bad that every morning the choir director, Dr. Nathan Carter, would call out in his gravelly voice, "Little Richard, you come sit in the front." He'd sit me right next to the piano, because I couldn't hear the notes.

He'd play a D. "Can you hear it?"

"Yeah." Then I'd belt out something very far from a D.

"Deeeeah."

"Da, Da, Da, Da."

"Deeeeah," I sang confidently, and looked at him.

He'd patiently say, "Okay, we'll try again tomorrow. Just relax."

I did get better. The better I was able to read music, the better I could put things together. Plus, I was smart enough to copy Dontae.

Choir was the first class of the day for all the music students. We began each morning singing together. It was church; it was communion. And because Nathan Carter was also the director of Morgan State University, which is a historically Black college, we learned a lot of Negro spirituals.

Ezekiel saw the wheel, way up in da middle of the air
Better mind my brother, how you walk on da cross
Your foot might slip and your soul get lost
Ole Satan wears a club foot shoe
If you don't lie he'll slippeth on you.

We laughed at the language. We knew people spoke that way, but to see it printed was significant. That language filled my head.

The choir performed all the time and all over the country, even at state functions. But we would sing anywhere. We formed spontaneous flash mobs and broke into song on the street, in the subway, and in the halls of school on any given day.

I started a running joke that became a spark for spontaneous music. I would say, "They looking for you."

"Who?" some unassuming person would say.

"Me boils," I would say, and then start singing, "Ding me boils— ding, ding me boils."

"What does that mean?" someone would ask.

"Ding me boils," I'd answer with a grin.

"But what's that?"

"Ding me boils."

"You keep saying the same damn thing. What does it mean?"

"It means ding me boils." We'd go round and round until I broke into song.

When something funny happened, "ding me boils" would reverberate through the halls. Real low I'd sing, "Ding me boils, ding, ding me boils," and then the sopranos and everyone would jump in. And we would have a spontaneous improvisation of "ding me boils."

Even the theater majors and visual artists wanted to join in.

"Will you teach me?"

"Yeah. You just go, *Ding. Ding.* You got it?"

"Oh yeah, I can do that." They laughed. Everybody had a part.

Performances were set off like fireworks. One person would start singing, then the choir would start singing, then Dontae would pull out his trumpet, and Eric and Kia and Matt would pull out their saxophones. There'd be a full-on jam session. We would be out, waiting for the bus, or going to the subway, or sitting in the cafeteria. Sometimes we'd perform during our practice period. Usually there was a hall monitor to make sure we were using the practice rooms, but when they were gone, we'd all flood into the hall and just jam. Or we'd sneak out a window onto the roof of the school and we'd sing to downtown Baltimore.

Once Dontae convinced me to play with him in the subway. He was a jazzer and I was a classical musician, so one day we were playing at the Rogers subway station. It is an outdoor station, nothing but a slash of gray concrete and a yellow line warning riders away from the edge of the track. Dontae and I took out our instruments and set our cases out to collect money.

"Yo, you play this baseline. I'm gonna play the melody."

I did what he said and we were playing for a bit.

Then some dude came up to us. "Yeah, man, that trumpet sounds good. But I don't know about that other shit, man. That tuba, now, what is he doing?"

Dontae took one look at my face. "Don't worry about it, man. I got you, man. I showed you how to play a really good baseline. What you did was right, man."

"Why would he say that? I played what you wrote."

"Yeah."

I left that subway station muttering, "I'm going to show that man. You don't make fun of the tuba. Why would he say that? I played the right notes, man."

"Yeah, it is supposed to go just like that."

"Well, what did you play, man?"

"I just played some improvisation on top of your baseline."

Most of the time, Dontae and I just hung out at his place on North Avenue. North Avenue had a hard reputation. I used to get off at the Mondawmin stop instead of at North Avenue because it felt safer. But inside, we could usually let the rest of the world fall away. We played Atari Pitfall! and listened to music. We had Walkmans and cassette tapes and lots of jazz and rap. Wynton Marsalis and Public Enemy and Erik B. & Rakim.

"Yo, you know the guys who fix the telephone wires aren't really fixing telephone lines, they're police officers?"

"What?"

"Naw, man, they watching the house. I heard my uncles talking about it." His North Avenue uncles were two known drug dealers in Baltimore. They never really talked to me other than to say, "What's up, shorty? Keep doin' that music." But I was always afraid that his uncles would get arrested.

Boom. Boom. Boom. Boom.

We ran to the window and Dontae said in a voice that was half scream, half whisper, "Get down. Get down. Get down."

"What?"

"Get down."

I looked over the windowsill and saw a person lying in the street and people running. We stayed there, crouched low. The police came and put a black bag over the person.

"Oh, whoa."

"Yeah, they dead, man," Dontae said, real quiet and slow.

I'd never seen a dead person. "Maybe they're going to take him to the hospital."

"Naw, man, when they put them in the black bag that means they dead."

I looked down at the bag and was overwhelmed by its color. It was the first time that black meant black to me—it wasn't a color or a shade of skin, black represented the end.

"We gotta go down there and tell them what happened."

"You crazy. We didn't see anything. Don't go down there. You might get shot."

Don't snitch. Don't tell. It's just not your business. I didn't know about any of that. What happened that afternoon stayed with me. I thought about the man who died on my way home. I thought about his dead body when I lay in bed that night. I thought about him when I played music.

"Wow, you saw your first person die at my house. How you doing?" Dontae asked the next day.

"Okay," I said, but inside I was in shock. I had witnessed a murder. I had seen a man lying in the street. It haunted me. He could have been anyone. He could have been Dontae. He could have been me.

That could happen to any of us, any day.

16

A Stranger in the Distance

I came through the door real quiet and tiptoed through the kitchen. Richard and Vivian had forbidden me from going to the party at Devonne's house—an old friend from Fallstaff Middle School. I'd gone anyway, sneaking out and catching a ride with Ronald in an old blue Cadillac. Just as I reached the kitchen nook, the lights came on. Blip. *Either that is God or I am really in trouble.*

Granddad was sitting two feet from where I was standing with a shotgun pointed right at me. A trickle of urine wet my tighty-whities.

"*You mama temper!* I coulda killed you, boy. What did we say? You don't go out."

I was trembling so badly I couldn't speak.

"Boy, I coulda shot you," he repeated, shaking his head.

I skulked off to bed, grateful he hadn't pulled the trigger. I hadn't even known that he had that gun in the house, but I didn't have a doubt about whether or not he knew how to use it. Granddad didn't play.

As a kid, I was always playing in the basement. Under the stairs was a little storage area. There was a gun in there I always thought was one of Ricky Jr.'s old BB guns, and a box. One day I rummaged through the box and found a stash of Granddad's old army stuff—a can of beans, Chiclets chewing gum, a roll of toilet tissue, and an army blanket. There was also an old black-and-white photograph. It was pretty gruesome. There was a head on a stick.

I slowly climbed the stairs and found Granddad in the kitchen. I didn't know what to say, so I just held up the picture.

"What is this? Why do you have this?"

He'd sat down across from me in the kitchen nook, a serious look on his face. Granddad had a sixth-grade education. Serving in the army had been his first job. He went to Korea, learned fluent Korean, and fought for our country. The picture I'd found was of the first person he'd killed. Shortly after that he'd been out on a mission and he got stabbed with a bayonet under his armpit.

When he healed, he told his commanding officer, "No, sir, I ain't going back out there." So they put him in the kitchen and he became a chef. I stared at the church-going, *mama-temper*-swearing, Kool-Aid-making, bus-driving, oatmeal-pie-eating man who had bought me my first trumpet and taught me how to tie a tie, and tried to imagine how he had killed a man and been stabbed and stood up to his commanding officer and fought for a country that didn't even guarantee him his freedom.

But as tough as Granddad was, when he encountered the police, he was petrified. Early one afternoon Granddad and I were sitting in the kitchen nook when the doorbell rang. Granddad looked out the window and saw two police officers. His face went whiter than a yard full of snow.

If I hadn't known better, I would have thought he had robbed a bank.

"Don't say nothin' 'less they talk to you," he said, real low.

"Granddad, why are you shaking?" I headed toward the door.

"Get away from the door, boy!" he growled.

"Granddad, we've got to open the door. You didn't do anything."

When he finally did twist the knob and ease the door open, he was silent. I waited a beat and when he didn't say anything, I said, "Hello, officers, how can I help?"

"Don't you talk back to the police, boy, you keep your voice down."

"Granddad, I'm just saying hello to the officers."

The police just stared at me with an odd look on their confused faces.

They explained that there had been a couple of robberies in the neighborhood and they were walking door to door to make sure we weren't leaving the front door open or the cars unlocked.

When they left, I turned to Granddad. "That wasn't normal, Granddad. I've never seen you that scared before."

He didn't answer me. Instead, he simply said, "Just keep your nose clean, Richard." His voice was quaking. There was no mistaking that to him this was a life-or-death encounter, but I had no idea why he was so shook, although soon enough it became clear exactly how dangerous the police could be, especially to me, a Black man.

I watched the video of the police beating down Rodney King at my house. I watched it at Dontae's place. I watched it in Craig's living room. Every time, I saw the hate course through the cop's body. Every time he raised that baton up and smashed it down. He wasn't there to protect and serve, he was there to destroy. Every time I watched, acid churned in my stomach. Rodney's body was ours—it was mine and Craig's and Dontae's and Ronald's and Brandon's.

I didn't know how to talk about my fear or how what happened to Rodney King was a reminder of what this country thought of us. But I listened to music that articulated all of that for me.

"Yo, all the stuff N.W.A was saying, it's true," I said.

"'A young nigga got it bad 'cause I'm brown,'" Ronald rapped.

Craig and I nodded.

"Yeah, it's true, man, that's what they're talking about, man. N.W.A."

"You better watch your back," Craig said when we left that night.

Granddad never sat me down and had a "you don't talk back to the police, you keep your place" conversation. He was born in North Carolina in 1930. He grew up in a time when lynchings were a clear and present danger. He'd lived through segregation. He'd drunk from the colored water fountains, sat in the back of a bus, and been kept out of places—restaurants, schools, stores—because he was Black. He dropped out of school in sixth grade and later joined the army. Then, he'd moved north to Maryland. As a boy, if he saw the police he knew not to go home. You steered well clear of the cops.

Our talk consisted of him saying, "Just keep your nose clean and stay out of trouble, boy," and me saying, "Yes, sir."

I hated that he called me boy. I tried to talk with him about it—the racism woven into the word, the association with slavery. Every time he said "boy," it grated on me.

"I'm not a boy, Granddad, don't call me boy."

"You're a man, right? You're a young man, right? Well, then you're a boy."

"Granddad, I'm being serious. It's not that simple."

"Get outta here, boy."

"You're not getting it. I'm serious. I'm upset."

But he wasn't going to talk about it.

It wasn't only the police and the word "boy" that Granddad didn't talk to me about. He didn't really talk to me about anything—about racism, or sex, or my plans for the future. He and Vivian provided for me. They loved me, but they didn't ever say those words, not even when I was small.

In middle school my Sunday school teacher had instructed us to go home and tell our parents we love them. Obediently, I marched in the door and told Granddad and Grandma, "I love you."

They both laughed.

"What do you want?" Granddad asked suspiciously.

"I don't want anything. At Sunday school they told us to come and tell you we love you."

"Oh, okay."

My mama always told me that she loved me. But we talked less and less. She was becoming a stranger in the distance. I saw her on holidays and sometimes on my birthday. She didn't have a home and it wasn't like I had a number where I could call her and see how she was doing. If she didn't call the house, I couldn't talk to her. I'd get updates from my cousin Tracey, who called to check in on me periodically. When I did speak to Mama, it was awkward.

"Hello, baby."

"Hey, Mama."

"How are you doing? How's school?"

"Fine. What are you doing?"

"Oh baby, I'm fixing my life. Working on getting a job and an apartment, and I'm gonna come visit you real soon." She'd stopped telling me that I was going to move in with her years ago, and the truth was that I didn't want to. Granddad and Grandma and Ricky Jr. and Angie and the house on Simmonds Avenue was home. I loved my mama, but our lives had spun so far away from each other. Now she was my mom and a stranger all at the same time.

Mama still promised me things. She promised to bring me a gift at Thanksgiving. I didn't need anything. I didn't want anything, except that I still wanted badly to believe her. But I never knew when she would come or what she would bring.

The year before, she had come over for Christmas. I opened the door to my mom and a little boy who wasn't any higher than my knee.

"This is your brother, William," Mama announced like she was introducing me to a neighbor's child.

I may have only talked to her every six months, but from what little I knew of kids, this guy was a lot older than six months and she'd never mentioned him to me. It was especially surprising given that Mama had always told me she couldn't have more kids. But by then I didn't have a lot of expectations one way or the other, and William was just another fact of Cheryl's Sandtown life.

"What's up, little man?" I nodded at the boy.

William ran around staring at the tinsel-covered tree, the twinkle of the colored lights. Grandma had toys and candy ready. I took him out to the yard and he ran around and played under the picnic table, and I thought of Grandpa Archie and Angie out here with me when I first visited the McClains.

This visit was real awkward and no one talked much. That's the way it was the following Thanksgiving too. Mom arrived without William and without the present that she'd promised.

We ate and no one said much, and when she hugged me goodbye, I was relieved. I never felt that I *really* belonged to anything other than the small family of my mom and me. But now I didn't even feel like I belonged there. I was tired of pretending that she wasn't going to let me down.

After Mama left, Grandma and Granddad disappeared and I was left alone doing the washing up. My hands were covered in soap when the phone rang. I heard Grandma answer it in her room. I finished up the dishes, wiped down the counter, Pledged the dining room table, and flipped the kitchen light off.

"Baby Ricky, come on in here," Grandma called. "We have something we want to talk to you about."

I thought of the phone ringing and fleetingly worried that someone had died. I worried that something had happened to Mama on the way home. Or that one of them was sick.

"We have decided we want you to call us Mom and Dad, not Grandma and Granddad," Vivian said.

My heart zinged against the walls of my chest. But I simply said, "Okay."

They nodded.

"Goodnight, Baby Ricky."

"Goodnight . . . Mom. Dad." I tried out the new names.

In my room, I lay on my bed smiling to myself. I really belonged here, and I wasn't going to let them down.

17

Us and Them

Ronnie Block was the superhero guidance counselor who helped me pick conservatories to apply to. I only considered schools I could afford to get to for an audition: Juilliard, Curtis, Oberlin, Eastman, Peabody, Manhattan, and New England Conservatory. Ronnie helped me fill out the form that allowed you to waive the application fee so I could apply to all of them.

I took Peter Pan and Greyhound buses and trains to the live auditions. In Port Authority, I saw someone drop her pants and take a piss as if she was in a bathroom. I saw rats the size of my cat. I walked from the bus station to Lincoln Center with a tuba on my back and ate the fattest sandwich I'd ever seen. I wanted to go to New York.

I was hustling and saving as much money as I could. I ushered at the Meyerhoff, I ushered at a movie theater, I was a stock boy at Caldor and Montgomery Ward, and I did whatever odd jobs I could. Chris Ford hired me, Dontae, and one of his nephews to pour a cement floor in his basement. We started with some dirt and gravel and wire fence and ended up with a beautiful, smooth concrete floor. I learned that you can do anything if you are willing to learn, to collaborate with others, to do the work to begin a task and see it through until the end. I had the power to make something for myself.

By my senior year, I'd woven myself into the Baltimore School for the Arts community. I did a recruiting trip to local middle schools. We played our instruments for all the students and told them about our experiences at BSFA. I looked at all those little kids and thought of Dontae and me picking the trumpet because it had three valves.

When we got back to school the whole building was buzzing.

"It's been a crazy day around here," Matt told me near the instrument lockers.

"What?"

"Yeah, the girls were fighting in the hall."

While I was taking the padlock off the wooden door of my tuba locker, there was an announcement over the PA system. "Richard White, come to the office."

I was used to hearing my name over the speakers in Mr. King's voice. I was used to being in trouble. But today, I knew I couldn't be in trouble because I hadn't even been in school. In fact, I'd been out *helping* school. So, I started thinking maybe they were going to give me an award . . . a tubist award, or something good. Something good was definitely going to happen. I practically danced to the office.

I walked into Mr. King's office and there were twelve girls, the head of the chorus department, the head of the music department, the dean of the school, and the president of the school. Then, there was me, facing them all.

Mr. King had a real serious look on his face. Before anyone could say anything, I jumped in: "I don't know what happened here, but I was out all day."

Mr. Moore started laughing. My eyes landed on Danielle; she was not laughing, none of the young ladies were. Mr. King explained that these young women had been screaming and fighting in the hall. Apparently, I had caused the fight. Mr. Moore asked each young woman to go around and explain why they were angry at me.

"Well, I used to talk to Richard, every day on the phone. He would help me with life and now that he's dating Danielle, he hasn't called me. He doesn't even say hello."

"Richard was my brother . . . ," Yazzy said.

"I thought he was going to prom with me," Tiffany said.

"I just never thought Richard would date a white girl," Shadina said.

"Man, he was my homie. He was the one who represented the Black people. How's he going to cross over and sell out like that, and date a white chick?"

BAM!

The teachers were baffled. The girls had all been blindsided. I had been too, in a way. I would never have dated a white girl. I knew I was not supposed to date a white girl and I had no desire to. Are you kidding me? Why would I do that? But Danielle and I connected and race went out the window. We were two people who liked each other.

It was the beginning of May and Los Angeles was in flames. We were all watching the riots on television. Every nerve was raw. The lines between us and them—no matter who the "us" was or who the "them" was—were growing into gaping chasms. Danielle and I may as well have stuck a lightning rod out the window during a thunderstorm.

All the racial tensions that ran through the school, unspoken, were crackling to the surface. But we were also still high school kids on the cusp of change, surging with hormones and facing the unknown.

Ms. Johnson was very compassionate and she embraced these young women and me and said, "Look, you all are going to have to learn to share Richard, can we agree on that?"

Mr. Moore looked at me and said, "Richard, some of us would love to have the problems you have." I felt like the Fonz on *Happy Days*.

Each of the young women had to go back around the room and pledge that they'd be nice and that they could share me. It felt a little silly and there was a lot of giggling. But the whole thing had me thinking about how important it was to stand up for what I believed and what it meant to have integrity. I lost friends because I dated Danielle. I also learned to value my friendships and to be kind. It costs nothing to be kind.

That afternoon we all laughed, but we also saw that moment for what it was—a clear message that we had to open up a dialogue. Dr. Simons called a mandatory assembly and had teachers and counselors on hand. This was unprecedented. The school had never had an assembly about a social issue in the wider world, but it was time. We realized that although we went to school together, we didn't know each other.

At the assembly, people spoke up about their experiences.

Every day I catch the subway and I've got to deal with the cops beating up the drug dealers.

There were some people who would just get in their car and drive themselves to high school every day and they realized, *I had no idea I am so privileged.*

I remember coming out of that meeting, learning stuff about people that I'd had no idea about. Seeing some of my friends as just angry, mean people, and then to understand, *Oh, you have to deal with that every day.*

For the first time, things that were thought in silence were said aloud, and rather than dividing along race lines, we became less fractured and more unified. I left that assembly feeling like I was a part of the Baltimore School for the Arts family, and that we all needed to protect each other, like family.

But as tight-knit as we became, that spring, we were all focused on what was going to happen next.

No matter what happened, Dontae and I would always be brothers. We'd been in school together since elementary; it was almost inconceivable that we'd be going to different schools now. We made a pact in the back of Steve Yankee's jazz band class.

"You'll go study jazz, I'll study classical music, and then we'll meet up and make a rap record."

"Yeah, man. We're gonna be millionaires before we're thirty."

I wanted to leave Baltimore so Peabody was out, even though David Fedderly taught there. I didn't get into Juilliard or Curtis. I did not feel comfortable at my New England audition; I thought it was a racist town and walking the streets, I felt like an outsider. I chose Manhattan, but even though I had a really healthy scholarship, when we crunched the numbers, Mom said, "You are not going to Manhattan, Baby Ricky. The numbers just don't work out."

So I went back to Ronnie Block.

"Hey, I want to go to Manhattan, but my parents say it's not afford-able."

She arched an eyebrow and with a mischievous smile said, "Well, let's call them. Let's play them against each other."

I had no idea what that meant. You can't just call people up and ask for money, especially not after they've already offered me thousands. There's no way. She was bluffing, just trying to make me feel better.

But I sat in the hard chair across from her and watched her punch numbers on the phone as she pressed the receiver to her ear.

First, she called Manhattan and said, *Well, he got such and such from Peabody.*

She listened and scribbled down some numbers. They'd raised the amount of the scholarship money.

Then she called New England and said, *Well Peabody and Manhattan gave him this and this.*

She listened and scribbled down some more numbers.

I was dumbfounded. White people know where the money is. It was crazy that Ronnie could find all this money, and it was even crazier that these predominantly white institutions wanted to give that money to me.

That afternoon I went home and said, "Mom, I got some more money from Manhattan!" We sat at the dining room table and crunched the numbers again, but life in New York City was just too expensive. Peabody started looking really good.

Someone at church told my parents that if I got a really good schol-arship at Peabody, I should call our House of Representatives.

"Call who? And for what?" We learned that every representative has scholarship money that no one ever uses. I wrote a letter and I got the money instantly. It wasn't even difficult. It put Peabody at a whole other level. I was going to go to Peabody, and I'd be able to live at home and commute. But Mom said, "If we get this money, then we'll work out the dorm situation. I think you should have that college experience. If we have to take out a loan, we'll do this."

Goose bumps covered my arms and I just grinned ear to ear.

18

Crossing Over

"Mom, please pass the potato salad." Vivian handed the bowl of creamy, yellow potatoes down the Christmas table.

Mama looked at me questioningly. "You mean, Grandma."

"No, they said I can call her Mom."

Mama's face twisted. The whole table got quiet. I looked from Mama to Vivian to Richard. I loved all these people and I didn't want any of them to hurt.

"You both are my mom," I said gently.

I clung to my memories of Mama, back when it was just her and me. She would always be my mother. But alcoholism is a disease, and while I'd been waiting for her to get better, I had crossed over into the McClain family. I had to let go. I loved Mama, I always would, but she felt so far away, more like a distant relative than a mom.

After Christmas, months passed before I saw Mama again. In June, I called around until I caught up with her so I could tell her about graduation. "I'm so proud of you, baby," she said, and that was enough.

But when the phone rang while I was at Aunt Margie's, I had a strange feeling in my gut. Margie was speaking in hushed tones and then she called me over to the phone. "Ricky, Richard and Vivian need to speak with you." Why was I always getting bad news at Margie's house?

I could hear the hurt in Vivian's voice when she said my name, "Baby Ricky." She took a deep breath in.

"My mama died." It wasn't a question. I'd been waiting for her passing since I had known what death was.

"Uh-huh," Richard said, "Your mom passed away."

Vivian moaned: "Lord give me strength."

It was too late for me to go to the hospital. Mama had been admitted for an asthma attack, but they couldn't open her airways. She had died trying to breathe.

My head swam. *I don't have a mom.* But then I thought of Vivian. *I do have a mom, a real mom.*

When I got home, Vivian was sitting in the living room rocking back and forth and saying, "Lord, have mercy. Lord, Lord, Lord," over and over. "Lord give me strength."

I knelt down beside her chair and put my arm around her. She cried hard into my shoulder.

Everyone apologized to me a lot.

"I'm sorry," Angie said.

"It's okay." I felt like I was comforting her. Somehow, I was not crying. I was not sad. The last fourteen years had prepared me. Little by little, Mama had been slipping away from me. Now, she was gone.

A few years before my mom died, Vivian had called me into the kitchen.

"Come sit," she commanded. I knew it was serious, because *come sit* is what they said after I had been whipped and they were going to tell me that they loved me and explain why they had whipped me.

I hadn't done anything wrong that I knew of. Though I had told Vivian that I wanted to see Mama and if she wasn't going to come see me, I wanted to go down to Sandtown to see her.

"I know you are tired of being let down. I apologize," she said gently. "We have fears too. We are afraid that when you get old enough you will run back to those streets, and we want you to be able to take care of yourself, should you decide to leave."

All they wanted was for me to be safe. That's what they had wanted for my mama, Cheryl, too. When I was small, I'd thought Vivian was mean to Mama, but now I could see that she and Richard were haunted by the fact that they couldn't keep Mama safe.

In the days after Mama's death, I was numb and blank. But Vivian, my other mom, who was always a rock, was broken. One night I stumbled into the kitchen for a glass of water and found her sobbing over the sink as she washed the dishes. Her whole body shook.

Seeing her cry made something deep inside me ache. But I didn't know how to ask if she was okay. I just turned around and snuck back to my room.

Maybe Vivian felt she let Cheryl down, maybe she wished she had done something differently, maybe she was simply sad that her daughter was truly gone. I don't know what she was feeling, but I could see as clear as day how much Vivian really loved Cheryl. Her grief shook her, and it shook me. She was my mom too, at that point, and in some ways, she was more my mom than Cheryl, and I didn't want to betray her by grieving Cheryl. But the truth is, at that time, I didn't know how to grieve Mama.

Mama's funeral was at Gillis Memorial.

I approached the open casket. Mama was wearing a shirt she'd had my whole life. It was silky and white with ruffles and a black ribbon flower in the front. Her hair was short with big curls, as it always had been. But she didn't look like herself. I touched her arm and it was hard as a rock and cold.

The whole world wavered.

I made my way back to the edge of the room, drank a cup of water, and pushed through the service. I don't know who was there. I don't know if anyone said any words. I didn't speak. I didn't cry.

I felt guilty, but tears didn't come. That night I called Dontae. "Yo, I didn't shed a tear at my mom's funeral."

"Oh, don't worry about it," he told me, "You'll cry later. You just haven't processed it."

I didn't fully grasp what he was telling me, but I sought understanding and convinced myself that when people die, they go to a better place. I had always been told that death was a good thing. I was Methodist. I went to Bible study. I went to church. I believed that there was a better life after this.

But I also believed that you have to get the best you can here in this world. There is no time to waste. We all start living and dying the moment we are born.

19

Bridging the Gap

I came to the dorms with a suitcase and a tuba. Other kids and their parents lugged in crates of belongings, extra pillows, feather beds, posters, and their computers. I didn't even have a typewriter.

Mom and Dad introduced themselves as my grandparents. "This is our grandson . . ."

The words stung. Why were they suddenly calling me their grandson? I had never been more their son than I was then.

When they left one of my roommates, Chris, asked, "So was that your grandma and grandpa or your mom and dad?"

I hesitated. "Uh, both."

I struggled through my academic classes. When I turned in my first history paper (I painstakingly wrote in legible print and paid a student to type my papers) my professor took me aside. He told me, "Honey, this is not going to do. This writing is really deficient."

Tuba had gotten me into the school, but those lessons didn't go any more smoothly. The Baltimore School for the Arts gave me a scholarship that allowed me to buy my first tuba, so I arrived at Peabody Institute with a Cerveny and Fedderly's sound in my head.

I walked into the monochromatic Peabody practice room for my first lesson. Fedderly gave me a small smile.

"Congratulations. Welcome."

"Thank you."

"I'm going to say something and I need you to hear it. In four years, I'm going to have to tell you if I think you can make a career out of this and I won't lie." Fedderly spoke in a soft voice, but I heard him clearly. My first thought after my first lesson was that I needed to transfer.

In our lessons, Fedderly would play something, and then I was supposed to play it back, like call and answer, but my recall was way off on basic things, like playing the rhythm back to him. I wanted to do what he said and I knew how many hours I was putting in, and I still couldn't do it.

He told me that there is a distinct difference between having bad rhythm and having never been taught to count. "You have never been taught to count," he said. I realized that every time I messed up a piece of music, it really was because I was guessing and not counting.

Fedderly taught me how to count. He eliminated my guesswork—but that meant it was up to me to do the work. Now, if I missed a rhythm, it was because I was choosing not to count.

His frustration was very quiet. "How many hours are you putting in?"

"I'm practicing three hours a day, minimum."

"And that's what you brought in here this week?"

A molten lump gathered in my throat.

At the end of the lesson, I closed the door behind me and let the hot tears run down my cheeks. My feet flew over the stairs, my head bent low so I couldn't see anyone and they couldn't see me. But I was far from invisible. I was six-foot-five and one of fewer than ten Black students at the conservatory.

On my good days I'd tell myself, *You're one of a kind, what's wrong with that?* But the truth was I was sad; I never felt that I belonged. Still, I was determined to show these people that I did belong here, that I had the goods to be at Peabody.

Although I often felt isolated at school, I was still in Baltimore, which meant that I could see my neighborhood friends and my uncle Ricky Jr., who looked at my life with a mixture of envy and awe. "You live down here in Mount Vernon. You go to this fancy school. You eat out every day. You go to concerts."

I understood what it looked like to him. I was being introduced to a lot of white friends and I was seeing a whole other way of life. They had cars and I didn't even have my license. They had a seemingly unending stream of cash from their parents and they had credit cards. I had no idea that you could take your parents' credit card and buy *whatever*. A credit card was a foreign and mysterious concept to me. *Oh, what? You just eat out every day and then you just pay this back later?* The next thing I knew, I had a credit card and was living a very different life. Ricky Jr. said I'd moved up and lost my sense of reality. But when I left my apartment and crossed the street, all the car locks still went *Click. Click. Click.*

One day a white friend was with me, and she looked at me and asked, "Did you hear that?"

"Yeah, that's my life. Let's go."

I looked into a little blue car trying to catch the driver's eyes, hoping to make them feel ashamed. I was used to it but it still hurt my feelings. Some things were never going to change.

My friend Raymond, whom I called Ray, started visiting me at Peabody. He was Anthony's cousin, and he was ghetto fab. He had jacked-up teeth, definitely from the hood, and the people at Peabody were fascinated by him, especially the young women. In some ways he was the bad boy; in other ways he was the monkey, the entertainment. He had nothing to do—he wasn't in school and he didn't have a job. I knew what kind of life he was living because he'd come back to school in the same clothes he'd been wearing the day before. At Peabody, he'd discovered a safe haven.

"Yo," I greeted Raymond good morning. He was lounging on the couch in my room.

"Yo, what's up with you today? I'm gonna just sit here and chill."

"Yo, I got to go to class. I'll holler at you later."

Later my friends and I would be gathered in the cafeteria doing our homework and Raymond would come in and tell some outlandish story that had everyone cracking up.

"Man, I gotta do this paper," I'd say. I did have to work, but I also wanted to get some space from Ray.

"Yo, forget that homework. Let's go get a forty. Cheers. Bottoms up." Everyone laughed.

We would go get something to eat and I would pay for him, or one of the girls would. "Yo, get me this time, I'll get you next time." But we both knew that he wouldn't.

Ray would hang out with me in dorms, and he was like catnip for all the pretty young women. He was so different from anyone they'd ever known. He was straight from the streets and he started hooking up with a couple of the women in my dorm. He moved from young woman to young woman, not speaking to them after, leaving havoc in his wake. It was bad.

The women kept coming to me and asking about Ray, wanting to know why he'd stopped speaking to them, or why I thought he'd done this thing or that thing.

"Yo, this is crazy. You gonna get *me* in trouble. How many women are you talking to, man?" I asked him in my room one night.

"Take it easy."

"Man, don't do that. Pick one girl and deal with her."

But he just kept at the game.

I was always on edge that he was going to embarrass me. I guess I was on edge about myself too. I wanted to belong, but I didn't really fit in with either side. My feelings about the whole situation were even more complicated because I was the president of Campus Crusade for Christ and Raymond wasn't staying the night so he could play Uno.

I was both friend and police. I got an earful from everyone. Peabody was a really small school. Everyone knew everything. It didn't help that Ray was really not supposed to be there at all since he wasn't a student. I was tired of trying to navigate both sides.

Then Ray broke a vocalist's heart. Someone started calling security on Ray, telling them that this guy had been hanging around and spending the night and they should make sure that he goes home at night or not let him in at all. When security found him, they escorted him out of Alcatraz, the walled section of our campus where the dorms were. It went from him being welcome to hang out, to someone calling security every time he showed up.

"But I'm here to see my friend," he told security. Then they called me and I had to vouch for him. It put me in an awkward position. Security started enforcing the rules—you had to sign your guests in, which made Raymond my responsibility.

Finally, after a few weeks, I said to Raymond, "You've got to go. You're causing trouble."

"What you saying, man? This doesn't have anything to do with you."

"But it does have something to do with me. I brought you into this circle. People are unhappy. Now it has to stop."

"Oh, I see you moved up, and you too good for us now?"

I bit my tongue, but thought, *This is not your playground. You don't belong here anyways.* I cared that he thought I was being uppity, *and* I didn't care. I didn't like the way Ray had treated people or how I had been inserted into his personal relationships by proxy, but he also represented where and whom I came from and I never wanted to turn my back on those roots, they are as much a part of me as my blood, my teeth, my skin. Raymond's presence threw my new life under the microscope and I realized I was always going to have to deal with making adjustments between worlds.

It wasn't easy to go home either. Even though I'd known Craig since elementary school and he was always a stand-up dude who helped me tackle my chores and had run for help when I'd lain on the football field unable to walk, hanging out at his house once I'd started at Peabody also had its complications.

We were sitting around playing video games one evening. I never once won. Craig would make fun of me. "Yo, you just keep trying, man. I kick your butt all the time, but you're always willing to play."

"Yeah, it's not like I'm going to be *penalized* for it or something."

Craig busted up laughing. "What? This fool just said 'penalized.' What does that mean? Yo, you're talking different. Yo, you're different, man."

"What? 'Penalized' is a normal word."

"No it ain't. Yo, daaaang, you different, man," he said again. "Yup. You not the same."

"How am I different? Because I'm talking proper?"

"Oh, look at that." He straightened his back and said in a stiff voice, "Because you're talking proper. Penalized."

"Whatever, yo, are we gonna play the game or what?"

"Yeah, we're going to play the game. I wouldn't want you to get penalized."

But I was, and as I defended myself, I felt the gap widening. I rode the subway back to Peabody feeling awkward and alone.

In the Peabody courtyard one morning, Dean Baxter asked me how I was doing.

"Not good."

"What's wrong?"

Worlds collided in my head. I had abandoned what I knew to become a stranger in a strange world. I didn't fit in anywhere.

"Nobody here looks like me and you guys don't care."

"I want you to see my secretary and schedule some office hours."

In the dean's office the next day I shifted in my seat, unsure what we were going to say to each other. But Dean Baxter jumped straight in. "So, Richard, what's going on?"

"I go to theory class and I'm the only Black person. I go to orchestra and I'm the only Black person. I'm the only Black person everywhere I go here. I don't see anyone who looks like me. It makes me feel weird."

"I can see how that would be weird. Are people being mean or disrespectful?"

"No. I just feel like I don't belong."

"Well, we need to figure out if that's our problem, or if that's your problem, or a combination of both. But this is worthy of us figuring out."

There were no Black professors. There was no Black student union. There was no Black representation anywhere. "Look, my friend can't even come here because you don't have a jazz program."

"Okay, but this is a classical conservatory."

"Yes, but classical music and jazz feed each other. Juilliard has both classical and jazz. Jazz is an art form, and by not having it here you're telling me that my music, my heritage, is not worthy of study."

I was offended. Peabody was the first music conservatory in the country, and here it is exclusively studying European music, as if American music is less significant. Jazz and gospel are the voice of America, how was the oldest American conservatory not with the program? Besides, whether we play jazz or European pieces when we play music, we are all playing the same notes—there are no notes set aside for Black people. It's music. It's universal.

No matter what you thought about the American-European musical divide, from a business point of view, Peabody's bias toward European music was hurting the program. They were overlooking all these admissions that could change the whole climate of the school, not to mention the richness that comes out of that kind of exchange of music.

Dean Baxter must have been thinking about what the expansion of Peabody's programs could mean, because he very quickly said, "There are going to be changes around here. Things take time. Thank you for expressing your concerns to me. I'm going to look into all of this."

After he met with the handful of Black students on campus, he told me, "We can do better and we will." He delivered. Pretty soon they announced that they were starting a jazz program. My everyday existence may not have changed immediately, but seeing the school take action and having Dean Baxter continue to check on my progress and well-being made me feel less disconnected.

By midmorning, I was starving. I had worked out and finished my first practice, and my stomach was growling. I opened our fridge—a jug of water. I opened all the cabinets—Swiss Miss cocoa. The only thing I found was a bagel that my roommate Chris had left on the counter. I ate it. I knew I shouldn't have. It was soft and chewy and I slathered it with butter.

When he got home, he burst into my room yelling.

"You ate my bagel." Spit sprayed off Chris's lips. "You don't know how hard it is to get food. This is not okay. My shit belongs to me. This shit belongs to me," he declared, waving his arms around the apartment we'd shared for a few months.

I was stunned. "Yo, it's okay. I'll go get you another bagel right now, man."

I heard him on the phone with his mom, and together they exclaimed over and over what an inconsiderate roommate I was.

I called Vivian to vent.

"What? Let me call him."

"Naw, Mom."

"We're coming down there right now. You get your shoes on."

I had no idea what she was going to do, but I was pretty sure she was going to blow some shit up. I didn't say anything to Chris. I just got my shoes on.

A few minutes later our buzzer rang. I pressed the intercom button and the static crackled out of the speaker. "We're here. You come downstairs."

Vivian and Angie were waiting in the car. We drove to the market.

"I'm gonna get a cart. Angie, you get one too." And then she turned to me and with ferocious sweetness said, "Ricky, get whatever you want."

I put a few things in the cart.

"Get two of them. Get three of them." She picked out things too and then, standing tall and proud, she paid for the two shopping carts full of food.

We packed the apartment with the groceries. There was so much stuff we had to put boxes of cereal under the couch. Loaves of bread on my nightstand. Little Debbie cakes in my closet beside my jeans.

As we shoved things into random crevices, Mom stuck her hand on her hip and warned, "He better not touch none of it." Then she looked at me. "You okay?"

I laughed out loud. "I am *more* than okay."

When Chris came home, he had calmed down. "I'm sorry that I did that, man." Then he looked around the apartment and added, "But your mom is crazy."

"Yeah, you better not tell her you ate any of this," I said, and then we shared some of my frozen fish sticks.

20

Brotherhood

Halfway through junior year, I got another roommate. Ricky Jr. came to live with me. In high school, after Vivian and Richard asked me to call them Mom and Dad, Ricky had joked, "I was your uncle, but I guess we're brothers now."

"I guess we are brothers now," I agreed, and we laughed together. When he came to campus that year, I introduced him as my brother.

Ricky Jr. laughed easily, he was sensitive, and he always told me he was going to leave Baltimore. Mom would say, "Ricky Jr. is a bum, he's got to go." Dad would say, "The only time Ricky Jr. told the truth was when he was sleeping." Ricky struggled with many demons.

When I was in grade school, Ricky's wife and he split up and he moved home. I didn't know then that he was addicted to heroin, but stuff started to go missing—money, my Transformers, and once he even stole a pot roast out of the freezer in the basement, so my Dad put a giant padlock on it.

Growing up, everything in the house was under lock and key. If you wanted a soda you had to go into my parents' room and ask for one from out of the closet. But even with the locks, stuff still went missing. One day while Mom and Dad were at work, I woke to a rustling sound coming from their room. I knew they weren't home and I knew that Ricky Jr. and I were the only ones in the house.

So, a few days later, when no one was home, I decided to try to pick their lock, and it was easy to do. I didn't tell my parents.

When Ricky Jr. and I were home alone together I would pretend to sleep, and he would open the door to my room and check that I was sleeping.

"You've got to stop taking from Mom and Dad, you're hurting them."

"I ain't do it. I'm telling you, yo, if I did it I would tell you."

I didn't believe him, but I wasn't going to snitch on him either.

My friends would come over and ask, *Why that big lock on your parents' door?* I'd have to explain. So my neighborhood friends started putting two and two together.

I never saw Ricky on the street, but my friends did, and they couldn't figure out why my uncle was homeless.

He'd sneak into the garage and sleep in the old car. My dad knew that he was out there; he didn't have the heart to put him out.

"Yo, they just kicked him out?" Ronald asked, not bothering to hide his disbelief.

"Yo, your uncle homeless, yo. I saw him sleeping on the bench," Craig said.

I understood why they'd kicked him out and I thought it was a mistake when they let him back in; I'd seen the devastation he caused them.

Chris and I still shared an apartment and my room was basically one giant studio entertainment center with a TV and a large couch, where my brother started to sleep. At Peabody, I was living the life Ricky felt he was supposed to live. I took him out every day. I had an American Express card, plus my parents gave me two hundred dollars a month, and I worked as a caterer at the Peabody Court Hotel. Ricky and I also got jobs at a for-hire security agency.

At one of the security jobs, we had to wear black pants and a white shirt. I threw on a tie and the manager liked it so much he made it the standard uniform.

"See, man, everywhere you go, you just change things. I mean, yo, you changed the uniform, now we looking all professional. It's cool." We felt good. We felt like we were rolling in it. I was saving money to help him get a deposit for his own apartment. He was on cloud nine.

One of the reasons I let him sleep on my couch was that I could watch him. He was far enough from uptown that he wasn't doing drugs. I had done the math in my head—I thought in a couple months he'd be clean and we could get him his own place.

"Yo, I'm going to get my life together. I'm forty years old and I just can't thank you enough, man."

Ricky Jr. taught me things too. One day he heard me on the phone with my little brother, William. I'd never really had a relationship with him, but since Mama had died, I felt tethered to him in this way that I couldn't explain. It was unfamiliar and foreign.

When Cheryl was alive, I rarely saw William and we never talked on the phone. But after Mama died, William had wanted something from me, something I didn't fully understand.

I had been nineteen when she died, and he had been eight. Our experiences with Mama were very different and we didn't have much of a relationship. He was a stranger to me.

But he would call me periodically. He called me at Peabody real upset, wanting to talk about the day Mama had died. He was really angry with me and looking for understanding.

"How could you not come to the hospital?" he demanded.

I took a deep breath. "William, by the time I knew she was at the hospital, she was already gone."

"But you didn't come see her."

I didn't know what to say. I'd gone to the funeral with everyone else. I hadn't gone to see her body at the hospital. I hadn't wanted to. When Vivian told me Mama had died, it was as if she had vanished completely. There was no one left for me to touch or hold or long for the way I had longed for her for so many years.

"She loved you," William had told me on the phone, his voice hoarse. I could tell that he wanted something from me, but I didn't know what. "You know, the last thing she said to me was for me to be like you."

"What? What did she say?"

"She said, 'I want you to be like your brother.'"

My heart stopped beating, the air stopped going in and out of me, everything was quiet. Before she died, my mom had been fighting for air. She used her last breath to tell William to be more like me. Chills ran up my arms and neck.

For the first time, I felt the need to connect with this young man. But I had no idea how. I didn't know how to deal with the weight or depth of having emotional feelings for William or Mama or my life in Sandtown. I put all that life and hurt in a box, like Richard's box from the Korean war under the basement steps.

I didn't know how to say "I love you" to William. But I knew how to give him a gift. I showed him love the way Vivian and Richard had shown me love—I bought him things. He would say, *I want a Nintendo*, and I would buy it. He wanted something and I wanted to give him something. So when Ricky Jr. heard me on the phone with my little brother, I was asking William, "Yo, how can I help you? What do you need?"

William told me about the kicks he'd been coveting.

"All right, I'll bring the shoes by tomorrow, man."

When I hung up Ricky said, "That ain't right. Why you keep buying him stuff? Why don't you just have a relationship with him?"

"You telling me not to buy him stuff, because you want me to give you the money."

Ricky looked at me, hurt. "Naw, man. For real, you should try to have a relationship with him."

One spring day I was about to run out to the store and looked on the entertainment center for the twenty-dollar bill I'd left there the night before.

"Check the kitchen. I thought I saw it there," Ricky called out as he looked under the couch.

I looked on the kitchen counters, in the junk drawer, and dug through the dirty laundry for the jeans I'd worn the day before.

"Maybe you put it in your shoe," Ricky offered. I hunched over my shoes and he said, "Let me check the closet."

I stuck my head into Chris's room, where he was hunched over his desk.

"Yo, man you see a twenty I left out yesterday?"

"No. Sorry." He kept working.

I gave up and ran out, but the thought of the lost money stayed with me all day like a wrong note.

When I got home I still couldn't find the bill. I asked Ricky Jr., "Did you take it? Just tell the truth. I won't be mad. I just want the truth."

He denied it.

"All right, man, but this twenty dollars better come up or you're getting out. Because I know you took it."

That afternoon Ricky Jr. was at work and my friend Ronald from home came over. I was still stewing over the missing money. I stopped midconversation and retraced my steps, lifted up the couch cushions, checked the bathroom. I wanted to find it. I wanted to be wrong about Ricky Jr.

I reached my fingers into the pocket of a coat that was hanging on my door. I touched the smooth, crisp bill and fished it out. A twenty!

"Ha!" I held it up triumphantly. The itch had been scratched. "Yo, I feel like a real asshole for being so judgmental. I just assumed he took it."

Ronald eyeballed me.

"Come on, man."

"What?"

"Yo, you know, you go to this fancy school but you stuuuupid, man. You don't got no common sense."

"Yo, why you calling me stupid?"

"It is ninety degrees outside. You didn't wear no coat yesterday, yo."

"Shit, yo. You're right."

When Ricky Jr. came home, I tried to get at the truth.

"Look, man, I know there's a problem here. I ain't mad at you. I need you to admit that you took the twenty and we'll forget about this." When he didn't say anything, I gave him an ultimatum. "If you don't tell the truth, then you can take this twenty and get out."

He stared at me for a long time. I could see him thinking about what he was going to do, taking my measure, wondering if I meant it. Then he said, "I didn't do it, man."

My heart fell.

"I didn't take the twenty bucks, but I'm going to take it now and I'm out." And he took the money out of my hands and skated.

From my couch I could see a bunch of bow-tie-wearing brothers in trench coats and aviator sunglasses on the roof. Chris pointed at the knots of traffic around the Peabody Court Hotel across the street from our place.

When I got to work that afternoon, my manager asked me to serve Louis Farrakhan. I wasn't a waiter, I was a busboy, but Mr. Farrakhan's people preferred to be waited on by a Black man.

So I walked up to the table of Black men in beautiful dark suits and bow ties. Seated with his security guards and assistant was Louis Farrakhan. He didn't speak to me. His assistant ordered oatmeal for him.

I put the orders in with the kitchen and when the cereal was ready, I carried it over on a tray. It was a round black tray with a white bowl of oatmeal, a small pitcher of milk, and a little white sugar bowl filled with tiny white crystals. Carefully, I placed everything on the table.

The bodyguards leapt out of their seats.

You would have thought that a rat had just run across the table.

"You've gotta get that out of here! What are you doing?"

"Nothing. Just oatmeal and sugar and milk. That's it."

"Don't bring any of the white stuff. You have to bring the raw sugar, the brown sugar," one of the brothers said.

I didn't know what he was going on about, but I understood that they preferred brown sugar.

"Don't you know?"

I just shook my head and glanced awkwardly at the group of bow-tied men. I fumbled the offending sugar bowl back onto my tray. *What would have happened if I'd brought them bacon?*

When Louis Farrakhan finished his oatmeal, he asked me to sit down and said, "Sir, I understand that you study classical music?"

I nodded my head, not knowing what to say.

"You know, I play a little violin. I'm learning Mendelssohn's violin concerto."

We talked about the beauty of music and melody, and I told him about my studies.

"We need more of our brothers and sisters doing this. Music is a healing source."

"Yes, sir. It is."

"What you're doing is rare for a brother." He looked me in the eye and said, "You're going to make a difference."

21

Truth Meter

I struggled to play low.

"This is not working. I need a new tuba."

Fedderly picked up my instrument and played the étude with grace and ease.

"Hmm. Same instrument. Same mouthpiece. Same room. Same chair. What's different?"

"The person," I said. *Shit. I don't sound like that.*

"Look, you come to these lessons every week, you're getting better. I'm proud of you."

I nodded, not trusting myself to speak.

"Don't backslide over the break," he said.

I still didn't say anything and he continued: "Here's the deal, Richard, if I pick up my instrument in your lesson, it means I think I can play it better than you. If you come to a lesson and I don't pick up my instrument or ask for yours, it probably means I can't play it better than you."

I looked into Fedderly's eyes and thought, *Well, I'm going to make it so you never touch that tuba again.*

After that, I didn't cry anymore. If Fedderly picked up the tuba I'd be like, *All right, next week I'm gonna do it better.*

I started recording myself and keeping a journal. The recording was my truth meter—it allowed me to be my own teacher.

At the end of my sophomore year Fedderly said, "You've outgrown this tuba."

When I explained that I didn't have the money, he told me we'd figure it out, and we did. We found a really famous Holton from 1912. That model of Holton led to the making of the York, which is the most sought-after tuba in the world. It was a singular instrument; it had been the influence for the famous York tuba owned by the Chicago Symphony. Playing a tuba with that much history was thrilling.

I felt like I was being initiated into a tribe. The tuba is the youngest of the brass instruments, invented in 1835, and since there is usually only one tuba player in an orchestra, we are a rare breed.

But the Holton tuba we'd found was a B-flat, and training to be an orchestra player, you play a CC tuba. Fedderly didn't flinch. "You have to get this. It is a great-sounding tuba. I think you can fix it."

So I bought a seven-thousand-dollar tuba for three thousand. I sold my Cerveny. I worked three jobs. I sent Bob Rusk fifteen hundred dollars.

Bob Rusk, who was the principal tubist of the Milwaukee Symphony Orchestra, converted tubas. He would take my B-flat Holton and transform it into a CC tuba. He took tubas worth thousands of dollars and cut them in his laundry room on top of his washing machine. His tubas were known as Frankenstein tubas—sometimes they had issues with tubing, but they sounded *really* good on certain notes.

I walked into the studio one day and found Fedderly in the little white room standing over a big box. Slowly, I opened the box. It had a gig bag. It was freshly painted satin. *It was fiiiiine.*

The tide changed.

Overnight I had moved from the smallest tuba you could play to the biggest. I was in love. My Frankenstein Holton had all kinds of problems, including some issues in the low range, but I just practiced. It made me a better tuba player.

I had been in band, which was the lowest ensemble, but when September rolled around and I auditioned for orchestra, Fedderly told me, "The conductor wanted to go with experience, so he let the older player in. But he said hands down, you kicked everybody's butt."

I didn't take it personally. I just wanted to be better. I had a tuba that had a voice. I had a tuba that could really sound like Fedderly. But class once a week wasn't enough.

Sunlight flooded into the atrium and I closed my eyes and listened to the sound of Fedderly warming up before his lesson. He was in a practice room off the atrium, so he couldn't see me, but I could hear every note he played.

He did Arban's warm-up.

"Hey, man. What are you doing?" one of the other brass students asked.

"I'm listening to Mr. Fedderly warm up."

He raised an eyebrow and headed off.

Fedderly finished one song and played the opening notes to *Meistersinger* by Richard Wagner. I picked up my little black notebook and marked down the song and made a note about how clear his articulation was. The beginning of every note he played was crystalline.

When his student arrived, I shut off my tiny black cassette recorder and went to go play everything I had just heard.

I sat in an empty practice room and lifted the Holton to my lips.

Be Be Be Beee Boooo.

I listened to myself. Replaying Fedderly's music in my head.

Be Be Be Beee Boooo.

I tried again.

Be Be Be Beee Boooo.

I played the tape once, listening with my eyes closed, and then I played it once more.

When I played music, the world receded. Music was all there was. I wasn't naïve enough, even then, to think that music could make race disappear, or that race didn't matter in music. There were very few Black students. There were no Black teachers. There was only one Black musician playing alongside Fedderly at the Meyerhoff. But the better I got at playing, the more the music moved me. For the duration of a concerto, I served the mission of a single composition. It was meditative. Reformative. It could transform the world and open another dimension where the complications of life and self disappeared.

My lessons with Fedderly went from him listing all the things I was doing wrong to him saying, "Thatta boy. That's it. You got it." He said "boy" differently than Dad. Fedderly pronounced the word as a celebration, and he'd pat my leg to let me know how far I'd come—how proud he was.

When he finally told me, "Yes, I think you can make it, and I think you need to leave Peabody," my heart ballooned in my chest. "I've taken you as far as I can. You need to go somewhere where you can reach the next level. You're done here."

I picked only graduate schools that had students who'd won jobs in major symphony orchestras within the last five years. I auditioned for Juilliard, Indiana, Michigan, and Northwestern. I got wait-listed at Michigan. I didn't get into Juilliard, again. I was offered an assistantship at Northwestern working with Rex Martin. That's where I was going to go. That was where Fedderly trained under Arnold Jacobs, and it is where most of the premier brass players in America went.

Fedderly and I were sitting hunched over his desk when I told Rex that I was coming. Another call came in, so I put Rex on hold and answered. It was Daniel Perantoni from Indiana University, calling to talk to me. I looked at Fedderly slack-jawed and he motioned to me to hear Perantoni out. I clicked back over. "Rex, can you hold on? Mr. Perantoni is on the other line."

I carefully pressed the Hold button, terrified I'd drop the call. *Click.* "Mr. Perantoni?"

"Look here, son," he spoke quickly, his voice warm and friendly. "We want you to come to Indiana. We thought of something special. I want you to go on tour with the Canadian Brass."

"With who? You mean *the* Canadian Brass?"

"Yeah. We're going to put you on tour. You're going to tour the country with them. And they're going to take care of your tuition."

I didn't know what he was talking about, but having my tuition taken care of *and* playing with one of the best brass groups was all I needed to hear.

Fedderly's eyes crinkled and a big grin spread across his face. I clicked back over to Rex. "Uhhh, Mr. Martin, Mr. Perantoni says I can come to Indiana and tour with the Canadian Brass."

Rex's voice boomed through the receiver. "I can't compete with Mr. Perantoni at Indiana. Either you want to come here or you don't. I can't compete with this."

I looked at Fedderly and pressed my hand over the mouthpiece. We had a little whisper. My heart was thudding hard.

Then I took my hand off the mouthpiece and said, "I'm sorry, Mr. Martin. I think I'm going to Indiana."

Fedderly leaned back laughing. He clapped his hands together noiselessly.

Then I clicked over and told Mr. Perantoni that I was coming.

Before I left for Indiana, I was going to play the Berlioz *Requiem* with the Baltimore Symphony Orchestra on the stage at the Meyerhoff. The *Requiem* uses four tubas, and Fedderly asked me and the other senior tuba players in the studio to play with him.

During rehearsal, I sat nervous and delighted. The brass choir was set up in the patrons' seats. The lights were hot, the stage shone bright, the wood of the hall glowed. I was right where I wanted to be.

Before the show that night, I saw Fedderly backstage.

"You ready?" he asked.

I wanted to cry and laugh and grab Fedderly and lift him up. Instead, I nodded yes and got focused.

Near the stage door I saw Dream Killer Manager, still wearing his J.Crew sweater and khakis. I was bigger and my hair was longer, but I watched him recognize me as I walked up to him carrying my Holton.

"Hey, man. Can you please bring me a bottle of water?"

22

In the Tuba Basement

Mr. Perantoni had wooed me to Indiana University by telling me I'd get to play with *the* Canadian Brass quintet. I had visions of being onstage with Chuck Daellenbach, one of the greatest living tuba players. I had fantasies of being "discovered," of fame and fortune. But my delusional dreams were efficiently extinguished on day one.

At our first training session, I turned to Dave, another tuba player, and asked, "Where's the Canadian Brass?"

"Oh, they're coming later. We're training."

I looked around and realized *I* was training with a drum corps. I mean, these people are marching *and* playing their instruments. I had just played with the Baltimore Symphony Orchestra. I went to a performing arts school, I didn't even know what marching band was, let alone a drum corps, which it turns out is a special marching band made up of brass instruments, percussion instruments, and color guard. I was green—I didn't understand the musical contributions of drum corps. To me, it looked ridiculous, something no self-respecting musician would ever do. Like circus animals—all the musicians get in costume, get in formation, and do tricks. Everyone wears a military-esque uniform and marches across fields during halftime at football games, in parades and civic events, in stadiums and arenas for competitions, and especially at the level of Star of Indiana Drum and Bugle Corps, they also make big money.

I wasn't the only one in shock at the first practice. Jerome Stover and Bryan Mack were two tuba-playing brothers whom Perantoni had also recruited for their tuba chops, *not* their marching acumen. We looked at each other, baffled. Three fish out of water.

This was like the military. Everything had to be uniform. We walked the same. We dressed the same. Everyone had a cooler. Everyone had a black towel. Everyone had white gloves. We all stood in a circle.

"Richard," Matt Harloff, the brass tech, said.

"Yes, sir."

"Do you see anything wrong here?"

"No, sir."

"You don't see *anything* wrong here?"

"Not at all, sir."

"Look at the person next to you."

I saw that Dave had a cooler, a black towel, and white gloves.

"Richard, do you notice anything?"

"Yes." I'm missing my cooler.

"You think we can fix this?"

"Probably not."

"Oh, you want to be a smart-ass?" He thrust out his arm and pointed. Everyone starts running. I just giggled. They ran half a mile and then ran back while I stood there, unmoving. They re-formed the circle and glared at me like they were about to cut my throat.

"Richard, when we mess up, we run."

"Oh, it's not smart to run with instruments."

Out juts Matt's arm and they all begin running again. I didn't move. So they ran again. As the herd ran back, a French horn player fell and crushed his instrument.

"That's why we don't run with instruments," I said.

Matt's face went a deep purple. "He has got to go. This isn't going to work," Matt shouted. All the staff shook their head in agreement. But, for better or worse, they couldn't get rid of me. Indiana University and the Star of Indiana were in the midst of creating a very avant-garde thing called Brass Theater, which was opera onstage, but instead of singers, there were brass instruments. To elevate the level of playing, they were recruiting musicians who could be part of Brass Theater—there were ten new recruits in the Star of Indiana. Well, when I woke up the second morning of training, there were eight. Jerome and Bryan were gone. They had fled back to South Carolina, as far from drum corps as they could get. But I was not going anywhere. The deal was I would do Brass Theater, and the Star of Indiana would pay my scholarship. If I did the Star of Indiana in the summer, they paid my fall tuition. If I committed to coming back the following summer, they paid my spring tuition.

I did the season and everyone hated me. Usually, if you join drum corps, you have worked really hard to be there and your parents have probably paid thousands of dollars to get you to this point. Here I was being paid to be there and resenting every moment of it. So I marched, but I marched badly. I didn't get better at following the rules either.

We toured all over the country, from Kansas to New York to Ohio. We'd perform in different gyms and the Canadian Brass would meet us there. Chuck Daellenbach was the tubist and a founding member of the Canadian Brass. When he played, the sound was rich and alive and it made the whole arena light up for me. All those years ago when Dontae schooled me at the Enoch Pratt Free Library, I'd looked up the Canadian Brass in the encyclopedia and seen Chuck's name, and now I was playing with him.

After the performances, we would pull out our sleeping bags and sleep in the gyms. The rules were clear: Do not bring food into the gym.

One night, I put some cookies in my backpack. Lying in my sleeping bag on the hard-ass floor, I heard a rustling.

Man, somebody's in my cookies. I turned around slow. I was about to jack someone up, stealing my cookies.

Rat.

"Wwwaaahhhh!" I screamed loud enough to wake the whole gym up.

"And that's why we don't bring food into the gym," one of the staff said.

"Okay. I got it."

The other musicians talked about me. *He's getting his tuition paid. He can't march. He sucks.* Then, we went into the recording studio, and everyone was messing up. The music director, Ray Cramer, expected a very high level from us and he was at the end of his rope and got a cold look in his eye.

He looked directly at me and said, "You, play."

I played.

The room got real quiet. The energy shifted.

I could hear someone behind me whisper, "Holy shit. He can really play." It was the first time I didn't have to play my tuba dancing like a monkey. I could just sit down and do what I do.

That fall we were also filming a PBS special to promote Brass Theater.

The Canadian Brass was very busy and they were clearly just learning the music. Chuck kept missing one passage. Ray Cramer looked at me and said, "If he misses this, I want you to come in."

"No way." *Not it. I'm not pinch-hitting for Chuck Daellenbach!*

"You know the piece, right?"

"Yes, sir."

"If he misses this again, I want you to play it."

I was scared out of my mind. Sweat was dripping down my back, running along the sides of my nose. The conductor raised his baton and we went. Chuck missed the intro to "Somewhere" in *West Side Story*. I came in. I caught the tuba player sitting beside me smiling.

As we filed off the stage, Chuck came up to me. "One, I'm impressed you had the balls to do that. Two, thanks for saving my ass. I understand you are serving time for a crime you didn't commit." We both laughed.

A few weeks later we were playing in the Great Woods Center for Performing Arts in Massachusetts. The audience was a sea of over twenty thousand people. The Canadian Brass were up onstage and Star of Indiana was marching in the grass in front. Between songs, Chuck pointed to me, called me onstage, and then stepped aside as I played one of the features with the Canadian Brass.

I felt like a rock star.

The Star of Indiana/Brass Theater tour was happening alongside me being in school. And at Indiana, there was no dodging academics. Expectations were high, and so was the competition. I went from the Peabody studio with three tubists to the Indiana studio with twenty-four. My first year, as I prepared for the school auditions for placement in a band or orchestra, Mr. P sat me down. "Look, don't be angry we've got some really good players, some really talented players. If you don't make an orchestra, you know, we'll just keep working on it."

I won a seat in the top orchestra and I started seeing players do things that I couldn't do. I was exposed to a whole other level of playing, which focused me. I went from practicing two to three hours a day to practicing five or six hours a day, no ifs, ands, or buts about it. I would wake up at six in the morning, hit the gym, and be warming up by eight. I would go to my first class, go home, take a shower, take a nap, come back and do an afternoon session, go to class, go home, come back and do a night session. I wasn't the only one doing this either. Sometimes I would get to school at 6:50 a.m. thinking, *Yeah, I'm the first one here,* and I'd walk into the music school and hear three other players already working in the tuba basement. They all got jobs.

The tuba basement kept you honest. Our giant tuba lockers were down there and originally the basement was just meant for storage, but the tuba players took over—we had a couch, a microwave, and a refrigerator, and we all practiced in the big open space. Some days there'd be ten people in the basement playing at the same time. One person would be doing scales and another would be working on a symphony. It sounds crazy, but practicing in mayhem makes you a better player. When I learned to play something new I was better at it because I'd heard it so many times. It also made us more competitive. I would hear people doing stuff better than me, and I would take notes on what I needed to work on.

Every skill I hadn't mastered was a tiny flame licking at me, burning, building toward a massive conflagration. I had to do more. Everything was riding on this. There was no time to waste. There was no good enough. There was no second best. I had to be everything I could.

I thought of Ed telling me that good tuba players didn't get jobs. I thought about the folks in Sandtown who hadn't gotten all the chances that I had. I thought of Mama, dying so young, leaving so much undone.

I wanted to check out of this world having put it all on the table— whatever the universe had given me, I wanted to be able to say that I had nothing left because I used all the talents and gifts the universe provided to the best of my ability. My mom's death taught me to get going, to count the seconds instead of the days.

I was twenty-three and had learned a lot about not taking life for granted. The spring before I left for Indiana had been full of such lessons, and there were more lessons still to come. The only thing that would stop me from succeeding at this point was death.

23

Life Is Fair Because It Is Unfair to Everybody

One morning before I'd left for Indiana, I was woken up by the siren ring of the phone. I fumbled the receiver to my ear. Ronald's voice was hard. "Yo, we gotta go beat some dudes down!"

"What are you talking about, man?"

"Craig got shot, man."

"What? You lie. You crazy, yo."

"He was at the gas station on Park Heights near Cold Spring and some dudes came in and tried to rob him."

We sat on the phone pouring our grief and fear into fantastical plans of revenge. But we weren't gangsters.

The next morning, I went over to Sinai Hospital. Craig was lying in the bed. He looked me in the eye and said, "Yo, I can't feel my legs."

When I saw his mom, Ms. Laura, her face was drawn and she looked older than when I'd seen her a few months ago. She hugged me tight.

His family had had it rough. When we were in middle school his dad had fallen asleep at the wheel while he and Craig were driving somewhere. His dad died in the accident.

"Yo, what happened?"

"Yo, they pulled up on me. I don't know what he got and he don't know what I got." Craig wouldn't give the dude his money and the dude wouldn't back down.

I didn't know what to say, but I had to believe that Craig would be okay. He had to believe that too. "You're going to walk again, you know. This is temporary."

A few weeks later I had another reminder not to take my time on this earth for granted. There is no way to pause life; anything can strike or happen at any moment.

"You need to come over here, boy. Your mom had a stroke," Dad said over the phone, his voice even and calm as if he weren't telling me that my mom might die.

I ran from my apartment around the corner from Peabody to Mercy Medical Center. We'd just been there earlier in the spring when she had quadruple bypass surgery.

Mom looked like a stranger. Her mouth was twisted. She was talking but I couldn't understand a word she was saying.

"Hi, Mom." I gave her a kiss on the cheek and said, "Everything's going to be okay."

The room was cold and filled with beeping machines and people who came and went like the tides. Her boss from the shipping and receiving department popped his head in to check on her. All the people Mom knew from working at Mercy for so many years seemed to stop by and wish her well. I held her hand and we sat like that for a long time watching the nurses and doctors come in and out, writing down numbers, taking her temperature, changing the IV bags.

I looked at Dad. "I'm not going to school. I'm going to call Indiana and tell them I'm not coming."

He ran his hands through his hair, which was white and pulled back in a small ponytail.

A tear rolled down Mom's face.

Dad looked at her and said, "I think she wants you to go to school."

But I couldn't imagine going all the way to Indiana when Mom was like this. I didn't want to lose another mother. After Vivian had asked me to call her Mom, my love for her and Dad exploded, like I'd been damming it up until I was given permission to love them as deeply as I did.

Over the next few weeks Mom got stronger, her speech got clearer, and we got to bring her home. But the decision on whether to go away or not was weighing on me. Sitting in the kitchen nook, I blurted out, "Mom, Fedderly told me that if I stayed home it would kill you faster."

"He's right," she said, real matter-of-fact. "I want you to go to school."

I did go to school and I worked hard. With Mom being sick and Craig getting shot—he had survived, though he still couldn't walk—I couldn't take anything for granted. But lest I forget that nothing was certain, the universe gave me another reminder.

That September the news was on while I was doing my homework. "Rapper Tupac Shakur has been shot in Las Vegas." He'd been shot before and I believed he'd pull through. A few days later his death was announced. I played his records all day for days on end. His picture was everywhere, but all I could see was the boy who'd taught me about Black Power and had me rapping at the cafeteria table. *Now we was once two niggas of the same kind*, ran through my head. He was gone; I was rattled.

It seemed like no one from my life in Baltimore was safe. It seemed like Baltimore wasn't safe. But Baltimore also felt very far away from my life in Indiana.

I must have grown used to living in a place filled with a lot of people who don't look like me, where people talk about distance in terms of cornfields instead of city blocks, because when I went home for Christmas my second year at Indiana, on the subway from BWI airport I caught myself thinking, *Man, there really are a lot of Black people*. Then, real quick, I fixed my face in case anyone thought I looked like a tourist with my suitcase, my tuba, and my shocked expression.

Mom was making her famous potato salad when I walked through the door. She held up her arms and gave me a big hug from her new wheelchair.

Dad said, "Hello, boy," which was as close as he'd ever come to saying "I love you."

On New Year's Eve, Dad fixed chicken, black-eyed peas, and collards. We watched the fireworks on TV, and then the news came on and they announced that Baltimore's first murder of the year happened at 12:01.

The news flattened the joy of the festivities. Baltimore was the murder capital of the country. This place was broken.

Then they identified the victim as Aaron Tracey Fair.

Tracey. My cousin.

I started to cry.

Back in Sandtown, Tracey and I had chased each other, played hot butter bean, and transformed my crutches into toys. He always knew where I was. Years after I left, he'd call me up. "How you doing, man? You doing all right?" He even came to the McClains' just to check on me. He wouldn't tell me he was coming, he just rang the doorbell, and when I answered, he'd wrap me in a big bear hug.

"How you gonna remember where my house is?"

"I remember where your house is, man."

He had just come home from basic training. We walked to Luckman, we were just catching up, and while we wandered through the park, he spat a rhyme: "East to the West, North to the South / Shut up homeboys 'fore I hitchu in the mouth."

"Yo, that's really cool, man. How'd you come up with that, man?"

That was the last time I saw him.

Now he was dead. He had two kids and his wife, Cassandra, was about to have a third. I wished I could switch places with him.

It wasn't just that Tracey was dead. Since Mama died, Tracey was my last lifeline to the world I had been born into. With Tracey gone, my family—the family I'd shared with Mama—had died too. That family was gone. My connection to them was gone. I was angry. I was defeated. All the mettle drained from my body. I slumped in the chair.

I looked at Dad. "Look, man, this is crazy. I'm off playing tuba and this is what I come home to. I guess I'll just stay away."

"You gonna make it. Keep going," Dad said.

"Baltimore ain't shit." When Ricky Jr. cursed, Dad looked at him funny.

"You'll be all right," Dad said, and urged me to keep studying.

We all sat together for a long while. We'd each known too many people who hadn't lived long enough.

The next day, I called Fedderly. "Man, I don't know if I should come home anymore."

"Why?"

"My friends come back to school telling me about their gifts and how great Christmas was, and I come home and my cousin is the first murder of the year."

He listened. When I was done, he quietly said, "I'm so sorry."

"I feel like I can't come back here. I feel like the city keeps warning me: This is what you can become. Like if I stay here, I'm next."

Everything I was doing felt insignificant. Playing tuba at university felt silly. At the same time, what else was I supposed to do? It's all bullshit. There's no reason why something is fair or unfair, but it is that way for all of us. Life is fair because it is unfair to everybody. You just have to keep on.

I felt heavy. I knew I couldn't go back to Baltimore. If I came back to this place, back to Sandtown, back to where I came from, I wouldn't survive. I was twenty-four years old and I'd known too many people who had passed to the other side, and whether or not that life was supposed to be better, I still had so much I wanted to do in this one.

I don't count the days ahead. I don't take anything for granted. I always feel incredibly behind. I always have to do shit now, because I could be checked out at any moment.

24

My Second Family

I didn't feel anger or bitterness toward the world, but it was abundantly clear to me that I was going to get knocked around by this planet and I better toughen up so that whatever hits me bounces off.

Whether or not I'd ever go back to Baltimore, the streets of that city were imprinted on me and the fact that I was a tall Black man didn't go unnoticed either. I'm sure my size got me hired at my first paying job in Indiana—a bouncer at a bar called Kilroy's.

Fights would break out and the bartender would call out, "Richard, we need you." I'd dutifully head over and then I'd get to the fight and find myself looking up at a massive football player.

"Maaaan, I don't know why they called me over here. I'm definitely not going to mess with you, but I'm supposed to come over here and tell you to stop."

"It's all good, dude. We don't want to get you in trouble."

Working as a bouncer wasn't my only job. I also worked as a teaching assistant for Mr. P. I taught the entire studio, even the doctoral students, in his absence. Mr. P saw the level that they came back at after they had worked with me and said, "You taught the kid to play like *that*? You did a pretty good job." He trusted me and so did the tuba players who all wanted me to hear them play.

I did everything I could for Mr. P. I would do chores. I would clean his studio. I would make little Post-it notes reminding him which students he needed to write recommendation letters for, and then I'd proofread the letters. I was his TA but I worked like the professorship was my job. Any way that I thought I could help Mr. P, I did. I inhabited the role, going so far as to regularly eat his lunch. Each day he put his lunch in the refrigerator at the studio, and each day I would eat it. He never complained. Then one day I sank my teeth into his ham and cheese sandwich and felt fire on my tongue, the inside of my cheeks, the roof of my mouth. He had loaded the sandwich up with the hottest peppers he could find.

Besides a lot of free lunches, I also got a tuition waiver, a monthly stipend, and health insurance, which turned out to be useful.

One afternoon when I was having an applied lesson with Mr. P, I told him I didn't feel well. I was out of breath, my head and chest hurt, and I had fever chills.

"You don't look good, son. You should go get checked out," Mr. P said, worry creasing his forehead.

"Yeah, maybe I'll go after class."

"No, I think we can reschedule. You should go now."

My friend BK took me to the hospital. A nurse drew some blood and asked me what my pain level was on a scale of one to ten. "Ten," I said.

They ran a few tests and everything came back normal, so they gave me a shot for the pain—in my butt—and sent me on my way. It left me loopy and temporarily improved, plus the idea of a shot in the butt made BK, Quincy, and me crack up. But once the pain reliever wore off, I knew I wasn't well. Mr. P and his wife, Judy, called every day, and when I didn't get any better after a week and a half, they called their doctor friend. When he found out they hadn't taken X-rays at the hospital, he got them done.

The X-rays showed that the sac around my heart was filled with fluid.

I was diagnosed with pericarditis and admitted right away. The hospital room was small and had a window without an inspiring view—no mountains, just the dark Midwest light bouncing off neutral walls. An old TV and me lying in that bed for two weeks.

Quincy came to tease me in my hospital room. "You got the carditis? Wow, that's serious," he said, having no idea what was wrong with me.

Mr. P was constantly checking in. He came and sat with me in the hospital and called all the time. He must have let my teachers know that my condition was serious, because everyone reached out to tell me not to worry about the work. One of my professors told the class that I was very sick and that I might not make it. All my classmates sent flowers and these emotional notes, saying that they would pray for me. Those letters rocked me, and for the first time since the whole ordeal began, I was scared. The seriousness of what had happened hit me.

I'd always been fascinated by the idea that we start living and dying the moment we're born. I'd known too many people who had passed on, and now I was facing the reality of my own life starting and ending the same way. But I found comfort in believing that every ending has a new beginning.

Thankfully, I made a full recovery, and weeks later when I was discharged, Mr. P gave me a big hug and said, "I knew you were going to be okay, son." His eyes were glossy with emotion. He and Judy invited me to stay with them, and even turned an extra room in the basement into a bedroom. But I didn't want to be a burden, so I went back to the apartment I shared with Keita Kimura and ate lots of miso soup.

Even though I never stayed in it back then, the room in Mr. P's house was always a topic of discussion. Mr. P made anyone who came to town and stayed with him, no matter how prominent a musician they were, call and ask permission to use *my* room. I still get calls from musicians saying, "Hey, Rich, I'm going to do a master class with Mr. P and he says I've got to call you. Is it okay if I stay in your room?" This was more than just verbally being part of the family—the room was a physical representation of my place in their home.

Although I didn't stay with Mr. P and Judy after I got sick, I ate dinner with them all the time. They always called when they were cooking one of my favorites, like spaghetti and meatballs. Mr. P would call me and say, "Rich, Judy got tons of food. Why don't you come on over to our spot? We'll take care of you. We want you to be okay." Sometimes Judy would get on the phone: "You haven't been here in a while and the candy dish is running over a little bit. Come over and get some candy."

Shortly after I returned to school, Judy was diagnosed with lung cancer. It was a hard time. Mr. P loves her like crazy and he was always by her side. By that point, I was back at school and work and I basically ran his studio so he could be with Judy.

One day after our lesson, I asked Mr. P how Judy was doing. Tears filled his eyes and he said, "She's got to make it, Rich." I didn't know what to say. Even though by that point I'd faced a lot of death, I had no idea how to console him. I just listened, and eventually Judy pulled through and beat the cancer.

Playing with the drum corps was my third paid job in Indiana, and at times it was even more dangerous than being a bouncer.

My second year with the Brass Theater, I inadvertently negotiated better terms for the entire instrumental cast. The Star of Indiana/Brass Theater CEO, Jim Mason, came to me at the end of the first season to lock me in for the next year.

"There's no way in hell I'm doing this again." They wanted to grow Brass Theater, to part from the Canadian Brass and replace them with a quintet from Indiana. They wanted me to be part of that.

"What would it take for you to come back?"

I thought, *There's no way you can get me to come back. Are you crazy?* But what I said was even more outrageous: "Look, man, I can't be sleeping on the gym floors. I need a condo or something."

"What?"

"I can't be playing music all summer, I need to be paid for my practice. I need a contract or something."

In my second summer, we were stationed in Branson, Missouri, and we all had condos, and everybody had some kind of contract.

There had been a cost, though. They did a show called *The Wizard of Oz*. I was the Wicked Witch of the West and I flew around like Peter Pan dressed in drag.

Mr. P, Mr. Harvey Phillips, and Dee Stewart all came to hear me play. Generally, I kind of winged it when it came to Brass Theater, but with those three in the audience, my performance was significantly better. One of my colleagues at Brass Theater heard me play that day and teased me, "Oh, we get it. We've been getting the B product." But no matter how well I played, when I came out in drag, flying across the stage, grasping my tuba for dear life, they lost it. Their laughter erupted loud enough for me to hear as I swung through the air. Though that humiliation didn't compare with what happened at another performance.

During one show I flew down upon the Munchkins, and then prepared to fly off. Only instead of a gentle whoosh of air ending in me offstage, I hear this country voice announce, "He ain't coming up."

I'm sixty feet in the air with a tuba, dressed in leopard skin tights.

"Yo, he ain't coming up for real," the country voice announces again.

The lady in the audience who is seated right below me looks up. "Lord, honey. Are you supposed to be right there?"

I can't talk. I'm about to pee myself. I just shake my head no.

I am not supposed to be right here. For the next half hour, the show went on beneath me as they tried to get me down. Finally, they hoisted me up to the landing and unhooked me, but I couldn't even walk because I'd been suspended in the air for so long the harness had left my legs two sacks of pins and needles.

I didn't want any part of this. I wanted an orchestra job. I did want the scholarship money *and* the salary I was paid for working over the summer, though. But if I was going to live in this state filled with white people and distance that was measured in cornfields, I was going to need a car. In Baltimore, public transportation had always been more than enough to get around, but after a year in Indiana, I called Dad and explained to him I would need a car.

The next time I was home, Dad helped me buy my first car with the money I'd earned doing Brass Theater. On the way back to Indiana, I decided to stop for the night in West Virginia. All down the strip, the motels had big lights flashing VACANCY. I pulled into the first one.

In the lobby, the security guard and desk clerk both eyeballed me. I asked them for a room for a night and the desk clerk said, "We don't have any rooms."

"Oh, well, the sign outside . . ." I gestured to the brightly lit word stretched beneath the motel's name.

"That's a mistake. No room." The security guard's words were clipped and there was nothing polite about what he'd said.

I drove down the street to the next motel with a bright VACANCY sign beaming, and this time the security guard didn't mince words: "Nobody in this town is going to have a room for you."

I booked it to my car and drove fifty miles to a BP gas station and slept in my Buick LeSabre.

25

Keep a Dime in Your Shoe

"Maaan, ramen noodles sure taste different when you're eating them because you want to as opposed to because you have to," Larry said.

I busted out laughing, "You got a point, man."

There were just six brothers in the Indiana music school. We introduced ourselves after an assembly where we had realized ours were the only Black faces in the department. I became really close with Quincy Roberts and Lawrence Brownlee, who were both in the voice department, and Weston Sprott, who was in the brass department—he played the trombone. Larry and I lived together in an apartment complex off Seventeenth Street.

When we'd finished our bowls of ramen, Larry said, "Man, we should join a fraternity, man. I'm looking at Alphas. Martin Luther King was an Alpha." He started looking up all these people who were Alphas on his phone.

I didn't really want to be in a fraternity. I certainly didn't want to be hazed. But I played along and looked up Kappas.

"I ain't gonna be no Alpha; they have honorary members." It didn't mean anything because someone can nominate you, but you don't have to do a thing. "I might be a Kappa."

A mentor of ours, Mr. Gordon, was a Kappa, and when Larry and

I told him we were thinking about joining, he was like, "We'll put you guys through, and we'll make sure it is done right." We were already in graduate school and Indiana did not have an alumni chapter and technically we weren't supposed to be allowed in, but Mr. Gordon looked at our résumés and put in a recommendation that we be allowed to pledge with the undergrads.

The president of the local chapter called and said, "You guys must have friends in high places because this has never been done."

We were allowed to pledge.

It was like the military. Hell, it was like drum corps. I resented it the way I resented having to play my tuba walking in a line stuffed into some stiff maroon-and-white uniform. The pledges had to do everything together—physically and mentally. If they told us to do something, they wanted us to use our brains. They told us to bring them fifteen hundred bucks. This basically seemed like extortion. I was pretty angry, so I gave them Monopoly money. Our pledging dean loved it and exclaimed, "That's what I'm talking about, that's how you're supposed to use your brain."

Another rule was that we were supposed to have a dime in our shoes at all times. I thought this was dumb and the dime was always sliding around my sneakers and annoying me, so the coin came out and I didn't think about it. But the president of our chapter did random spot checks and one day he lined all the recruits up—Larry, me, and a bunch of eighteen-year-old brothers, and instructed us to remove our shoes. Everyone did, and sure enough, everyone but me had a dime in his shoe.

"You just killed your brother," said the dean of pledging.

"Come on, man. Shut up." I thought this whole charade was ludicrous.

Then the brother sat me down. "Do you know why you're doing this?"

At that point, I was doing it because my best friend was doing it.

"You know why this fraternity was started?" he asked, clearly expecting me to answer. When I shook my head no, he told me that the fraternity was started because brothers were being lynched in Indiana. Then he told me that the Jordan River that runs through campus, if you were a Negro, you weren't allowed to cross that river. You had to walk all the way around campus to get to class. The hatred ran so deep that in Indiana, some African Americans were forbidden from entering the classroom. Instead, they had to sit outside and listen to the class.

Men always needed to have a dime so they could go to a phone booth at any moment and call for help. They created a fraternity, a house where they could live together so no one would ever have to walk to class alone, a house where there would always be someone to answer the phone.

I knew that history wasn't truly behind us. During my first week in Indiana, I was walking along Kirkwood to the square down near city hall when I turned a corner and found myself standing a few feet from a group of more than thirty men wearing white hoods and chanting. There were no police and everyone was walking around as if this was normal. *Where have I come to school?*

It turns out I was in school thirty minutes from Martinsville, home of the Ku Klux Klan, and a rally with men in full hoods was a perfectly acceptable expression of freedom of speech. There was a dull thrum of men yelling and throwing their arms in the air. I didn't wait to hear what they were saying, or what they thought of me. My heart thudded in my chest and my stomach dropped. My instinct was to run. I started moving, fast, somewhere between walking and running. I was gone.

But the specter of the KKK was always present. In one of the lecture halls was a mural by Thomas Hart Benton that depicted a KKK rally—hooded Klansmen and a burning cross. The hate hung around us and it wasn't distant history.

So when the dean of pledging broke down the significance of the dime, his words landed. I felt them in my chest. I felt all the Black men who had been here before me. I felt all our history. The way we had been kept out and kept down. It felt like a minor miracle that I had been saved the night of the blizzard, that the McClains had taken me in, that I had picked up a trumpet and found the tuba and waltzed into the Baltimore School for the Arts. But there was another miracle—that I, a Black man, was here at all. Suddenly it felt of the utmost importance that we honor that and protect each other. As a Black man in America there is always a target on your back, regardless of how much money you make or what success you achieve. It is permanent.

This was not hazing. There was nothing that was going to cause me to die. This was a pledge. I was pledging to be part of the brotherhood. All of us are better than any one of us.

You can just go to the graduate chapter and pay your money and not go through the process of *becoming* a member, but then you are not truly one of them and they have a special name for you—paperface. I wasn't going to be a paperface. Larry and I were going to be made. To do that, you had to know your history. If you couldn't, you had to do calisthenics. They wanted us to understand that nothing that they could put us through was as intense as what the brothers went through before us just to get to class.

I pledged Kappa Alpha Psi.

26

On the Road Again, Businessman with a Tuba

"We gotta go to the tuba ranch and clean," BK told me in the tuba basement.

"For what? I'm out, yo. I ain't going to the tuba ranch."

That was blasphemy. "Do you know who Mr. Phillips is?"

"Yeah, but I didn't come here to clean his ranch."

"Well, we owe him everything."

"I don't owe him shit."

I thought we were going to come to fisticuffs.

"I can't believe you just disrespected Mr. Phillips like that. You don't say things like that about him."

"Are you kidding me?" I straight up started laughing.

I went to Mr. P and asked him what the deal was.

"Yup. You're in the studio; you go to the ranch."

Harvey Phillips had been the tuba teacher at Indiana before Mr. P. He was a pioneer who had changed how tuba was played and heard and celebrated. He created Octubafest, TubaChristmas, Tubasantas, Tuba-Company, and TubaJazz—contagiously joyful tuba playing that brought music to the people. He was tuba royalty. And after two-plus decades developing the tuba studio at Indiana and funding a scholarship, the entire department was loyal. Even though he was retired, he still created a world of music for us—with lessons, performances, and inspiration—and in return, the scholars of the tuba studio worked on the ranch, like monks at a monastery performing their tasks, an exercise in Zen.

That Saturday, the entire tuba studio piled into a half dozen cars and drove out to the ranch. There was the main house, the garage, acres of land, miles of fence, and an old-school gas pump.

This was the first time I'd been on a ranch. Or a farm. Or any kind of habitat with nature. I saw a big pile of manure. "Whatever dog dropped that pile of dung, I'm out of here."

"It's llama poop." BK laughed.

"They got llamas? Where are we?"

Mr. Phillips wheeled out of the house and greeted us. He was jolly, with big black glasses, formidable jowls, and white hair—he reminded me of Santa Claus, but instead of a sleigh full of gifts, he was doling out chores from his wheelchair. Well, really, his wife, Carol, doled out the chores.

"BK," she said, "please cut the grass."

"Bill, move the hay."

She pointed at me and sent me off to paint a fence. Bill said he'd rather cut the grass, and BK said he'd move the hay. Painting sounded a lot better than either, so I grabbed a brush and a bucket of paint.

I was feeling good. The sun was bright. I could breathe out there. *Up. Down. Up. Down. It's all in the wrist.* I made myself laugh, then stepped back to admire my work. I already had a beam and a half painted on the fence.

BK, who grew up on a farm, took one look. "Are you kidding me? You've spent two and a half hours on *that?*"

He grabbed a mop and started slathering it on the fence. "It is a fence, fool. Paint the fence!"

"Oh, paint the fence with a mop. Ain't nobody say, paint the fence with the mop." I was out of my element.

"I got this, man. You just go help with the hay."

I walked upstairs to the top of the barn. "What you all doing?"

"We're moving hay here." BK pointed to a spot just beside where the hay was stacked, then handed me a shovel.

"What? I thought we were gonna be moving the hay?"

"Yup, we are moving the hay."

"What? You're moving the hay one inch?"

"We gotta move all the hay so we can put it in there and it can slide down."

"Yup, this is why I came to Indiana. Just to be a city boy on the farm baling the hay. I feel real good right now." Everyone started laughing, and then we moved the hay one inch.

If you were a tuba player you were part of Harvey Phillips's family, you were part of his tribe. After chores, we ate chili sitting around the Phillipses' table. Mr. Phillips loved pickled herring, porter beer, and the good life. He had a table in his kitchen with a lazy Susan, so that if you wanted the potato salad, you just waited till it revolved around to where you were sitting. His house was also filled with music. He would play old recordings and there was a basement full of records. He even had music framed on the walls signed by composer Alec Wilder, who had been a dear friend of Mr. Phillips.

The ranch was a place of joy and possibility and when you arrived, those feelings were contagious. If Harvey dreamed it, he believed it was possible. He gave me, and everyone who worked with him, a sense of belief that the tuba could do whatever you wanted it to. It could be anything. He empowered us to believe that the tuba was magical.

Mr. Phillips had heard me play at Octubafest. He fell in love with my sound, and that was just about the highest praise I could get. "Oh, that sound! Way to anchor, Richard." He requested that I play contrabass tuba for Tubasantas.

In rehearsal at city hall he said, "That's it. You all listen to Richard. That's the sound we want."

While I was starting to find my voice on my instrument, I still had to make money as a bouncer. Then, one day, I was walking through the bar when my carpenter pants snagged on a nail on a bench. *Riiiiip.*

Are you kidding me? I didn't have the money to pay for a new pair.

Linda, my boss, told me she would buy me new pants, but I walked out of the bar knowing that something had to give. I had to quit. I might end up eating ramen, but either I would make money playing tuba, or I would stop altogether.

Indiana State University in Terre Haute had a tuba job opening. Mr. P warned me that they wouldn't give it to someone with as little experience as I had. I was only in the first year of my master's. I ignored him. I was still mad about my pants. Mad that I didn't have any money. Mad that I couldn't purchase a new pair. I applied and got invited to take the audition. I won the job. I became the adjunct tuba professor at Indiana State University the first year of my master's.

Then the Terre Haute Symphony Orchestra had an opening. I practiced and I won that. I was riding high.

I was working so much, I thought I might be able to go straight from getting my master's to getting a tuba-playing job, but Mr. P had different ideas. He wanted me to get my doctorate.

"I don't think I want to get a doctorate. I just want to practice and get a job."

"Before you make a decision, let me ask you a question," Mr. P said. "What are you currently doing that you couldn't do? If you started your doctorate?"

"Nothing."

"Okay . . ."

"Yes, I'll enroll tomorrow."

I did enroll in the doctorate program, but some part of me was still operating on the assumption that I would get a job with a top-fifty orchestra before I got my doctorate. When I was at the ranch, Mr. Phillips and I had long conversations about music and careers, and whenever I was wrangling with a big decision, I'd talk to him. I talked to him about whether I should play in orchestra or teach.

"Well, I don't understand why you have to choose."

He was right; I could do both.

"Richard, although you are a tuba player, it is important to remember you're in the business of music, so you should treat this like a business."

He told me about Big Red Liquors, a massive Indiana chain. Before Big Red there hadn't been a store that only sold liquor. "I tell you, Richard, this is the secret: If you want to be successful in life, find something that is needed that doesn't exist and then do it. You're a businessman and you're in the business of music. Everything you don't take advantage of and everything you can't do is a deficiency for you."

The world shifted. Possibilities for a tuba player were very limited, actually. Possibilities for a businessman with a tuba: infinite.

"Yeah, you know, I'm teaching at Indiana State, and I think I'll do it for a couple years and then leave."

He peered at me through his thick black-framed glasses and asked, "Leave? Are you ready to leave?"

"In a couple years, I think so."

"Listen to me, you're never really ready to leave a state until you can say you did everything there is for you to do. Can you say that?"

I went home and looked up every orchestra in the state of Indiana. Though I started playing with all the regional orchestras like Columbus and Terre Haute, I wasn't getting hired at Indianapolis Symphony Orchestra, the big dog. But one day, I would. Over the summer, I printed their season and practiced every song.

The next summer I was at the Spoleto Festival in Charleston, South Carolina, when I got a call.

"Can you be here tomorrow for ten o'clock rehearsal? We're playing Tchaikovsky's *Romeo and Juliet*."

I said, "Yes."

I hadn't gotten to that piece yet, so I listened to it the whole car ride back to Indiana and showed up ready. After that, they called me whenever they needed a tuba player, and I started doing studio recording with them. I, the guy who couldn't read music all those years, was a studio musician, a job in which all you do is sight-read.

I studied and practiced and pushed myself to excel, and after almost a decade of study, I felt I was ready to try out for a professional orchestra. The Indianapolis Symphony had a tuba opening.

When an orchestra needs to a fill a spot, they hold auditions, but until you're in the union, you can't just show up to audition unless you are invited, and even once you're in the union, if you express your interest in a job, you may get a letter advising you not to bother auditioning. Technically, you can still show up, but you've been warned that it will be a waste of your time and money.

Mr. P believed in me. He called the Indianapolis Symphony and told them they should see me, and I received a letter of invitation. I felt ready. I'd picked Indiana in part because their program had a history of students winning jobs in major orchestras. Our classes were designed to drill you into audition shape.

At Indiana we had something called repertoire class, or rep, as we called it, which is where all the students who are ready to get a job meet and play for Mr. P and all our peers and then are judged. Everyone tells you what you sucked at, and if you really ragged on someone, it was going to be your turn to play next, so you had to have your stuff together. Sometimes professionals would come through class to train for an upcoming audition.

One day Tony Kniffen walked into rep class. He was principal tubist of the Honolulu Symphony and was famous for having won the Chicago Symphony at eighteen and then being told he couldn't have the job because he was too young.

Mr. P set up a mock audition with current students and lots of alumni. We got dressed up, then we all lined up and one by one we played the excerpts Mr. P had set on the music stand in the center of the room. I played and I felt good. Then I sat back down and Tony walked his tuba to the chair.

When he set his lips to buzzing into that brass mouthpiece, I heard tuba like I had never heard tuba before. I didn't know the excerpts could sound like that. His notes were even and perfect. His phrasing was immaculate. Every sound reverberated in my body.

There wasn't any point in auditioning—*unless lightning strikes him, I am never going to win.* Still, I drove up with Brett Stemple, our four tubas in their hard cases piled in my Buick. *You must take chances. If you don't, you can be assured of one thing: You definitely won't win.* I told myself that I *could* win. Tony could have a bad day.

I took a chance. I was green. I didn't know the excerpts I was asked to play in the audition. I played them on a tuba that wasn't professional quality, a tuba that didn't even have all the notes. I didn't make it past the first round.

Tony did not have a bad day. He was amazing. He won. I did walk away with something though, I left knowing what you must sound like to win, and I knew that I could make the excerpts sound that way if I practiced enough. I asked Tony if he would give me lessons.

We met in the basement of his house. In my first lesson he ripped me a new one. I played for him and he said, steel in his voice, "Sure, you can decide not to learn how to do this thing that I can do. You can decide not to learn how to do that other thing that I can do. But I might decide that I want to leave Indianapolis. And then I might show up for the audition you're going to, and I *can* do all these things. Who do you think will get the job?"

I sat there, chastened. It was like Fedderly all over again.

Tony warned me: "One mistake is bad. Two mistakes is very bad. Three mistakes is catastrophic."

I thought back to the excerpts I'd tripped over at Indianapolis. I'd made at least seven mistakes. Damn. I was so angry and so motivated.

I didn't go back to Tony for another six months. I practiced every note that I had a problem with. I started with low F. *If it takes me three months, that's all right, I'm gonna go to E. Then E-flat. Even if I have to do every note and it takes a couple of years, I will own every note.*

When I told Professor Edmund Cord, the trumpet teacher, what Tony had said about making mistakes in auditions, he said, "Look, you can take that any way you want, but here's the reality of it: When you get dismissed from an audition in the first round, it is not because you missed a note. It is because of the seven other things you did before you missed that note."

My head was spinning. "What do you mean?"

"Listen, if you want to get to where you've never been, you've got to start doing the things you've never done."

I stayed quiet.

"Do you practice every day with a metronome?"

"No. Most days," I said, and shrugged.

"A tuner?"

"No."

"You need to have a metronome and a tuner out at all times," he instructed. "Do you have a list of your weaknesses, the things you have to fix for each excerpt?"

"No."

"You don't even have a journal?"

"No, sir."

I started keeping a journal and I broke my playing down to a science. I went from having 150 things to fix to really getting it down to one or two. I also read a book by Don Greene, *Audition Success*, which advised breaking up the excerpts into three categories. Category 1: Things you know you can't play. Category 2: If the sun is shining just right, your feet are feeling good, and you've had your favorite coffee, you probably could pull them off. Category 3: Things that you own that you can play no matter what.

Over the next few years, I worked to move all the excerpts into category 3.

When I went to the Indianapolis audition, I probably knew three out of the twenty excerpts they asked for. That meant I had to learn seventeen new excerpts and play them competitively against thirty to forty musicians who had been playing those same excerpts for the last ten or fifteen years.

Back at Peabody, Fedderly had expected me to play an étude like him, because it is an étude, a lesson in technique and mechanics. I was learning by doing exactly what Fedderly did; he was the expert. But mastering an excerpt is something you do over a lifetime—when you've truly mastered your instrument, your playing takes on a life of its own and you develop your voice.

My little brother, William, was developing his own voice too. One evening, he called me and we got to reminiscing about our cousin Tracey. I wasn't particularly close to William, but he'd call every now and then and I kept buying him stuff—I still hadn't found a way to follow Ricky Jr.'s advice and forge a meaningful relationship with him.

"Do you remember how Tracey could freestyle?" I smiled to myself.

"Yeaaah, man. Hey, you know, I'm battling."

"Really?"

He spit a dope rhyme for me.

"That's a freestyle?"

"Yeah."

"That's bullshit. You wrote that down."

"Naw, man. That's fresh off the dome."

I challenged him. "I want you to rap about donuts. You ain't got no words that rhyme with donuts."

He did it.

"Awwwwww shiiiiiiit. You're really making that up."

William had a lot of talent. He was offered a record deal when he was sixteen, but his dad didn't want him to live that life at such a young age. Though who knows what would have happened if he did. Not taking the deal certainly hadn't kept him away from street life. But the way things worked out, other pathways of possibility opened. That's the thing, if you push yourself, hone your craft, and stay sharp when opportunity comes, you will be ready.

When I went back to Tony, he told me I'd improved, but I was still not on the level. He wasn't done with me. He pointed at my Holton and said, "You've got to get rid of that goddamn thing." My Frankentuba had taken me through Peabody and through my first years at Indianapolis. But Tony hated my homemade, put-together tuba that had changed my life. He wasn't the only one. Mr. Perantoni had a fit one day in one of our lessons. "I'm tired of this damn tuba! Throw it in the trash can. Do it now."

I didn't know what to do. I didn't have fourteen thousand dollars for a new tuba. I called David Fedderly. "Hey, I need a tuba and I need it now. I'm done playing this one."

"I kind of knew this was coming," he said.

A few days later, he called me. "I'm going to be in Cincinnati at a brass conference. There's a tuba for seven grand. You can probably sell your tuba for close to four grand. I'll let you pay monthly for the remaining balance."

I got a gorgeous PT-7 and all the problems that I had playing in the lower register went away. Tony's work with me was deepening my understanding of what I was learning from Mr. P, and suddenly all my work was beginning to click into place. I'd work with Mr. P, I'd work on my own, I'd have a lesson with Tony, and when I had my next lesson with Mr. P, he could hear the difference.

27

Play It Again, Prometheus

When you took a lesson with Tony, he didn't charge you, but he gave you a CD or a book to read at the end of the lesson and you had to promise to listen or read. Tony had struggled and found real peace in faith, and he wanted to engage all his students in thoughtful, provocative conversation on all manner of things. The first thing he gave me was *The Secret*. The next book he gave me was about evolution. My talks with Tony confirmed my thoughts on religion, that people turn to religion because it simply makes their life better. They reach a certain point or a hardship in their life that they can't explain, and they turn to something bigger than themselves for the answer. I had stopped going to church but was deeply spiritual, and over the course of many lessons and many conversations, we bonded.

Tony called me up one day and offered me his ticket to a historical simulation of slavery at Conner Prairie, outside Indianapolis. He had to go out of town and he wondered if I wanted to go with his family. I didn't fully understand what it was, but pledging had got me thinking more deeply about history, so I said yes.

My only relationship to Conner Prairie was playing with the Indianapolis Symphony when I subbed for Tony. We would play summer concerts to thousands of people sprawled across the beautiful grassland as far as I could see.

Once I played a Fourth of July concert at Conner Prairie. I have an opinion about America's Independence Day: It most certainly is not a day of independence for my people, and I might protest in my heart, but I was being paid to do a job and I aimed to impress.

The musicians' entrance was hidden at the end of a long back road. As I pulled up to the security booth, I saw a few of my colleagues in the orchestra go straight through. But when I pulled up to the booth wearing the same clothes as them with my big tuba in the back seat, the security guard stopped me.

"Do you have a badge, sir?"

"No. They didn't give me a badge."

"Hold on, please," he said, and held up his hand.

"I know they didn't have a badge either. I'm here to play, man. How would I even know to come to this back road?"

He made a call. "I've got Richard White; he says he's playing the tuba for the symphony."

He hung up the phone and waved me through. The next day, there was a picture in the paper and there I was, the substitute tuba player with my cornrows and tuba, the only African American on the stage.

The morning of the reenactment, I woke up in the Kniffen house and Tony's wife, Amy, made us breakfast and made sure everyone had gloves and hats and proper shoes. It was cold and she knew part of what would happen would be outside.

At Conner Prairie there were people everywhere; it was like going to the movies, everyone milling about, tickets in hand.

We started out with a film that showed Indiana being a free state and the whole slave history, and then they passed out these white flags and said, "We're gonna go on a walk along the Underground Railroad. If at any point it's too much for you, raise the flag." *Why am I going to need a mercy flag?* I thought, but I didn't have time to dwell on it because after that, the world was not the same.

We walked downstairs and we were on the trail. It was dark and cold.

"Get in line, Negroes." Those words cut me, but I filed into line. We all did.

"Boy, get in line," a man spat his words at me and liquid hit my face.

"Oh look at this buck," one of them said, eyeing me up and down.

"Uh-huh. She'd be good for breeding," another man said, gesturing at the woman beside me. Three or four people threw their mercy flags. Amy looked pale, I thought she might throw her flag, but she didn't.

My stomach lurched.

"You go here. You go there." Roughly, they pushed people into two lines.

"I want you to pick up the wood, put down the wood. As you pick up the wood, you need to say, 'Pick up the wood. Put down the wood. Pick up the wood.'"

Someone fell. Someone was crying. Someone held up their flag.

There was a group of Amish people with us. In the midst of picking up the wood someone had actually knocked an older Amish woman on the head and she was bleeding. She didn't quit though.

As we were picking up and putting down the wood, Tony's son, Jason, wasn't doing it fast enough. They made him stop.

"You pick up two pieces of wood," they said to another man. "And you"—they turned to Jason—"say, 'It's all because of me. It's all because of me.'"

I wanted so much to save him. I wanted so much to protect him. But I worried that I was going to get us all killed if I did that. The whole experiment became real.

We fell back into line and they screamed at us, "Keep your hands up and your head down. You don't look nobody in the eyes."

A Black woman came up to me and said, "I need you to keep your head down." My brain was jacked up. She was one of them.

A white man walked over and looked at my ring and demanded, "Are you a thief?"

"No, sir."

"Are you telling me that your family is rich then? How can you afford that ring?"

"Family heirloom, sir."

"So, you're a thief since your family ain't rich."

There was no right answer.

We walked and walked. We walked until we were rescued by people working along the Underground Railroad. They hid us in a barn with stacks of hay, the smell of horses, and a bone-chilling cold that made my knees ache as we squatted on the ground. They began to read scripture and tell us how they were risking their lives trying to save us.

As we left the barn, they told us not to stop or talk to anyone. But as we were walking, a white man with a rifle appeared.

He told us he was a hardworking person, a good man who had lost his daughter on this journey, and that he could not get a job because everyone used slave labor rather than paying. He said all this with his gun pointed at us. Then he went to go get rope and we had a discussion about whether we should stay or run. I knew I wasn't staying; I didn't care what anyone else decided to do. So together we left to go back to the trail. As we walked, two people were kidnapped. I thought about throwing the flag but didn't.

A young woman was crying, saying, "I don't know where my cousin went. . . ."

We stopped at the home of a Quaker family. They read to us from the Bible and fed us cornbread. Then we met a Black family who gave us some nasty cornbread. They explained that even though they were free, they were trapped—too afraid to show their papers lest someone decide to rip them up, disappearing their hard-won freedom with a few quick flicks of a wrist.

At first, I had wondered why people didn't just rebel, overpower the slave owners, and rescue their families. But I was beginning to see that there were violent and terrible consequences for your loved ones. If you tried to run away, your family could be killed or sold apart or beaten because of what you had done. It didn't matter how strong or smart you were, there were no right answers.

I wasn't shocked. I was born Black in America. I was born in a neighborhood where everyone was struggling—with poverty, with addiction, with lack of opportunity—and in that neighborhood there wasn't a white face to be seen. I knew about injustice, prejudice, systemic oppression—but I had never thought explicitly about the way the slave owners turned love and community into a tool for oppression. Yes, you could love, you could have children, you could make a home, you could make music, you could learn, you could harbor beliefs. But if you stood up for yourself or anyone else, if you challenged the power structure in any way with a look, or a laugh, or words, or a rhythm, if you tried to run away, if you tried to exercise your autonomy, the people you loved could be hurt, or killed, or sold away. They used our very humanity to hold us in the most inhuman condition.

Afterward, there was a decompression session. Everyone looked stunned. Tony's oldest daughter, Evelyn, wrapped her arms around me and hugged me tight.

The ride back to the Kniffen house was awkward. Every time I looked at Jason, I thought, *Damn. If this had been my son, I wouldn't have been able to help him.* That haunted me. We all cried. By the time we got back, I felt scooped out. Humble in the knowledge of how much I did not know.

I felt the injustice of America's history every day in a thousand tiny ways, from the clicking of car door locks when I passed by to being stopped by security guards and police to arguing for a jazz program at Peabody. But never had I been able to truly imagine the experience of an enslaved person, or the way those experiences have branded us and our country in the centuries since 1619.

All of that history is tied up in our notions of independence and identity, freedom, and of course, race. Years earlier I had an argument about race with another brother. He told me, "It is all about education and money. If you're successful and you're well off, they don't see you as being Black."

"Excuse me?"

We debated intensely.

Finally, I said, "I need you to roll your shirt up."

"What? Why?"

"Roll your shirt up, man. Look at your arm. You are Black. You are never going to change that. I can't believe we're having this discussion."

"You just don't get it," he said, as if I was the one missing the point. Invectives were ricocheting off the walls of my brain. I wanted to argue, but what else could I say? No matter your education or your wealth, you cannot erase the history that has shaped this country. Race fuels everything about the way our world operates.

Maybe that guy really didn't see color, but I can tell you I sure did. And color was especially evident in the classical music world, where it was so notably absent. I'd gone from almost never seeing a white person other than the police in Sandtown, to being one of the few brown kids in the TWIGS program, and one of the few brown kids at Peabody, and now I was one of the few Black men in the Indiana music school, and I can tell you representation matters.

In the classical music world, there are so few people of color. When I saw other Black people performing classical music, I was awestruck. The first time I met Manny Laureano, who is the principal trumpeter of the Minnesota Orchestra and a brother, he had a fro and I thought he looked like Shaft. He had come to the monthlong National Orchestral Institute (NOI), on the College Park campus of the University of Maryland, to teach us . . . yoga. All I could think was, *Man, that's some bullshit. We don't do no yoga. We don't do no breathing, man.* But then I heard the man play and he sounded amazing. *If this yoga and breathing stuff can make you sound like that, then show me.*

He had us stand next to our chairs. We stretched, went to a quiet place in our minds, breathed. He took my mental focus to another level.

His lessons to quiet my mind were valuable, but it was the very fact of his particular existence that stayed with me. I'm always impressed when people from underrepresented groups participate without having to adapt or compromise. Here was Manny, who was so utterly himself. He didn't have to wear a costume—he didn't change his clothes or his speech or his rhetoric. He was hip. If I had not seen Manny, I probably would have taken out my cornrows and cut my hair before I went on the audition circuit, but he showed me I could be me.

Learning to be myself and to play the way I play was one of the hardest lessons of all. Before I could even think about being me in an audition, I had to get on the level. William VerMeulen, who was also at NOI that year, was the principal horn of the Houston Symphony. I played *The Damnation of Faust* for Bill in the master class as the entire orchestra watched. When I set down my tuba he said, "Okay. Now I know why you make zero dollars a week and I make thousands of dollars."

Shiiiit.

I started shaking. I pressed my hands into my legs so that no one would see the trembling.

"Look, here's what you need to do: Aim high. Break records. Do it now. You have to fix this. You have to know that you are going to win. When I took the Houston Symphony, when the finals happened, I showed up in my tuxedo because I wanted them to know that I was already dressed for my position."

He was telling me that I needed this kind of confidence. "You question yourself too much. You've got too many excuses. You have to know that you can play."

I nodded my head, not sure what I was supposed to do or say.

"So how are you gonna play?"

"I'm gonna do my best."

"No. Wrong answer. How are you gonna play?"

"Great."

"No. Wrong answer. How are you gonna play?"

"I don't know."

"You're going to play the way that you play. And that's what you need to be able to say. There's no guesswork here. When you can say, 'I'm going to play the way that I play and it's on the level,' *then* you are ready."

I went back to Indiana on fire. I was going to get an orchestra job. I started taking auditions—any audition that opened, I'd take. With each one, I mastered more of the excerpts. Then I went to Rochester and Albuquerque, but I could not get out of the first round. I'd rage that the auditions were bullshit. I'd despair that getting an orchestra job was impossible. I didn't know what you had to do to get out of the first round. What I did know was that I hated auditioning.

These weren't auditions; they were cattle calls. They'd herd us into the warm-up room, me and thirty or seventy or two hundred other tuba players all auditioning for the same job. Then we'd all start practicing. Most people were bothered by the noise, but I had trained in the tuba basement, so hearing everyone playing around me didn't bother me one bit. But that didn't mean I wasn't nervous. My heart started beating louder than a police siren.

When I walked into the warm-up room, I drew my group number and eventually me and nine other people would go onto the audition stage together and sit behind the black screen. We'd play one by one, five excerpts in five minutes, and then we were told if we would advance or go home. I was always sent home.

When I got back from auditions, people would ask, "How'd you do?" and again and again I would have to explain that I didn't win.

I told a classmate about how nervous I'd been and he told me he used beta-blockers. They reduce your blood pressure by blocking the effects of adrenaline, so your heart beats more slowly and with less force. I was a little dubious about putting a chemical into my system. I didn't have my first drink of alcohol until graduation night of Peabody because I was always fearful that I would share my mother's fate. I was uncomfortable taking a drug, but the beta-blockers don't allow you to do anything you can't already do. They just allow you to play the way that you play in the practice room. I took some and at my next audition I was calm and focused, but I still didn't advance.

A spot in Boston opened up. Everyone wants Boston. But if you're not qualified, you have to send in a tape. They had to listen to 172 tapes. They picked three. My tape was one of them.

I went there. I played. They didn't hire anyone. Then they did the whole thing over again.

I sent them the same tape. I got in the second time too and went to the live auditions again. Making it that far in the auditions for the Boston Symphony gave me credibility in my own head; I knew that I was on the level and that I could do this. After that, I started advancing consistently. I advanced in Milwaukee. Honolulu asked me to fill in for my friend Dave Saltzman, who took a leave of absence. But they wouldn't fly me back to the mainland for other auditions and when I looked up the price of milk and saw that a gallon cost seven dollars, I thought, *What, they expect you to live under a coconut shell?*

At Indiana, I took auditioning orchestral repertoire class with Thomas Robertello, who was a flute player. He talked to me about auditioning strategy. He told me to just lay low the first round. Don't make any mistakes. Don't do anything too much.

"Man, why would you lay low? You gotta bring your best, you gotta bring it," I argued.

Robertello was teaching me how to stay in the competition as long as possible. I had never thought about it that way. One day in class, Chris Lee and I were laughing about something and Chris exclaimed, "Holy shit, man."

Mr. Robertello took offense. "Oh, how dare you be so vulgar in front of me and the ladies." Forget all the dudes in the class—just him and the ladies. We laughed even harder.

He punished us by making us play every day. We would play and be eviscerated. And then the next class we would play again and be torn apart all over. We were like Prometheus, eternally tormented. Only we got better and I started coming to that class thinking, *I dare ya'll to say anything today.*

Part III

PATHWAYS OF POSSIBILITY

The New Mexico Symphony Orchestra invited me to audition again in 2004. I wasn't planning to take the audition because I was making more money doing studio work in Indianapolis than the NMSO would pay me. My goal was to get into a top-twenty orchestra and to get paid a living wage salary. But Jeff Anderson, who had been the principal tubist of the NMSO for fourteen years and had moved on to be the principal tubist of San Francisco, called me. "Look, I heard you are sounding really good. You have to take the audition. I told them that you would come through."

Again, I couldn't even afford the plane ticket and I couldn't go back to Mr. P. The parents of my friend Michelle Auslander, who was a singer at school, paid for my ticket to Albuquerque. My roommate, Keita Kimura, auditioned too.

We had a layover in Phoenix. I was really thirsty and we walked into one of those little airport stores.

"What? A bottle of water costs five dollars!"

Keita tapped me on the shoulder. "Richard, it's the desert."

I about fell down laughing.

Keita and I shared a hotel room to save money. The morning of the audition, I worked some olive oil into my scalp and cornrows. I put on black pants, a red shirt with intensely emotional faces printed all over it, and my red shoes that looked sharp with the red and white beads in my hair. I was ready.

The last time I had auditioned here I knew maybe ten of the excerpts, but now I knew all twenty—no, I *owned* them.

There were forty of us auditioning for the position. Ten were already crowded into the practice room, blowing on our tubas. Kurt Civilette, a horn player for the NMSO, led the first group out to the stage. It was Kurt and his big, toothy smile who announced the six candidates who would advance to the next round.

"Keita Kimura advances to the next round."

"Richard White advances to the next round."

Keita-san and I nodded at each other, and then I stepped outside into the desert heat and called Mr. P.

"We both made it to the semifinals." I tried to hold my hope in check, but Mr. P was optimistic.

"You're going to win, Rich; I have a good feeling about this one."

The New Mexico Symphony had grown since my last audition. They had their own space now. We weren't auditioning in an old church but in their facility with offices, rehearsal spaces, and practice rooms with gray squares of soundproofing mounted on the walls.

In the semifinal round, I was cool. I was flowing. I felt good. Kurt came back and announced the names of two other people and then he said, "Richard White will advance to the final round."

My heart skipped a beat. For the first time, I had made it into the finals. What if I never got to the finals again? I needed to win. I wanted to win. I wanted this job. I remembered Fedderly telling me, "You only have to win once. I've only won one more job than you." I wanted to never audition again. I started practicing, but it didn't sound like I was going to win. It was baaaad. I missed everything.

Kurt poked his head into the practice room. "Richard, you're up." He walked me to the stage. I walked slow, monitoring my heart rate.

I sat down. The screen was hanging in front of me, an endless expanse of black.

"The music is on the stand. Please play the correct order," Kurt whispered.

I began to play and it was magic. Everything was working. I didn't miss a thing.

I walked offstage.

When I saw Kurt again he said, "We're going to have a finals final." That meant an unscreened round.

He led me back to the rehearsal room. The black screen was gone and I could see the auditioning committee perched in their chairs. Their jaws clacked on the floor when I walked into the room—a brother with cornrows, red shoes, and my crazy red shirt. It took some willpower not to call out, "Surprise!"

I sat down and played the selected excerpts while they scribbled notes. When I stopped playing, it was quiet except for the scratching of their pens.

It came down to me and Scott Beaver for the section round, where you play with the trombone section. I went first.

I took a deep breath and we began. But Byron Herrington, second trombonist, was subbing on bass trombone, which is a different trombone from the one he usually plays, and he was not in tune.

I looked at him and said, "Should we tune, and play that again?"

He smiled at me. "Why, yes, we shall."

We played it again. Then I went and sat in the waiting room.

Scott came back too. We waited awkwardly until Kurt came into the room, his dazzling smile even wider. "We would like to offer the job to Richard White."

28

You Only Have to Win One

I wanted to jump up and down and yell, but I held it together. Then Kurt took me back to the rehearsal room to meet the auditioning committee: the conductor, Guillermo Figueroa, the trumpet player Jon Dante, the horn player Peter Ulffers, and the trombonists Byron Herrington and Debra Taylor.

Jon Dante looked at me with his hard blue eyes. "I've been doing this *a lot* of years. We have heard a lot of tuba players. That's the best freaking audition we've ever heard."

"I was looking at your résumé. . . . Not many people put their height and weight on their résumé. Six-foot-five, two hundred and fifty pounds. I was wondering if you were going to look like a linebacker," Peter Ulffers said. I laughed.

"I hope you come. Are you going to come?" Byron asked.

They seemed concerned that I might not take this job.

When I walked out into the bright sunshine, Keita-san was waiting for me. We hugged and he kept saying, "Wow. You did it!" over and over again. I called Mr. P and he was ecstatic. Then I called David Fedderly and thanked him. He said, "You did the work."

When I got back to Indiana and people asked me about my audition, I got to say that I won. Mr. P gave me a big hug and all my classmates were jubilant. One of us winning a job was a good omen for everyone. From my circle of African American friends, I was one of the first to do this.

"Oh, you won't stay there long, big things are for you," one person after another said to me.

Before I'd gone, people had been asking, "Why are you taking that audition?" I had turned down Honolulu and Austin Peay State University in Clarksville, Tennessee. I couldn't afford the Honolulu job and my experience during my interview at Austin Peay led me to believe that the music department was not very diverse, that the job was a minority appointment position to fill a quota. But that job would have paid me $42,000 just to go in one day a week. The NMSO was paying around $30,000 to be a principal player. It was a great gig to land—a one-year contract with a great orchestra, although it wasn't a job in the top-twenty orchestras I had dreamed about.

But Mr. Phillips was in my head. I was a businessman with a tuba. This was an orchestra job, which was what I wanted, and I had a business plan. I was going to get to New Mexico and get hired by the Santa Fe Opera and also teach at the University of New Mexico, and be earning more than I could make working in a more prestigious city with way higher living expenses.

When I told other brass players my plan, they would cock an eyebrow at me, or say, "Are you crazy, fool? No one who was there before you was able to do that, and they all left for bigger gigs."

No one else was me. No one else had a doctorate—or *almost* had it.

The summer of 2004 I arrived with my job at the NMSO and I simply called the Santa Fe Opera up and said, *Hey, I'm here. I would like to come play tuba for you this year.* They said, *Okay. We know who you are. We want to hire you for the season.* Then the university called and asked me to come in and talk. When they heard I had the opera *and* the symphony, they offered me a job as an adjunct tuba teacher.

I said, *Okay, but I can only do this a little bit because I'm so busy.* They gave me six students.

I flew back to Indiana every two or three months to work on my doctorate. I finished all the coursework before I came to New Mexico but still had the recitals, exams, and the dissertation. I took minor field tests and major field exams. I got to the point within the first year of being in New Mexico that I was an ABD—all but dissertation—and I sat on that for years. The doctorate was really only useful for teaching and I wasn't interested in teaching—it was a means to an end, and I was going to leave and get a bigger job, and then I wouldn't need to teach.

But in the back of my mind, I kept hearing something Mr. P said to me after he watched me teach one of his undergraduate classes. "Look, Harvey told me this and I'm going to tell you this: It is meant for you to teach."

The tuba studio was a closet. When I first walked up to it, I noticed a small hole in the door and a tiny sticker that said: TUBA. The room was not worthy of the sticker.

I put a little desk in there facing the small window and waited for my first student.

Jordan Sayre walked into my closet office, took one look at me, and said, "I don't know you. Who are you? Where are you from?"

"Excuse me," I said, hiding my amusement that he was greeting his new professor with such dubiousness. "I am Richard Antoine White, principal tubist for *your* New Mexico Symphony Orchestra and your professor."

"Okay, man, that's cool."

When I came to UNM, there were what we called six-year seniors: students who took five or six or seven years to graduate. The school had basically given up on them and decided that this was too long to take for a degree, but I saw something different.

Jordan Sayre and Antonio Romero had both been at UNM for six years by the time I came. They were both first-generation college students. Jordan was from Aztec, New Mexico. I've driven past Aztec—there is nothing there. It is a little Western ghost town. Antonio is from Albuquerque. They were two typical New Mexico kids—they grew up in families and communities with low education, and just by being here they had beaten the odds.

Working their way through UNM, they had never had anyone *really* believe in them. This also meant that they hadn't had anyone who took them seriously enough to have high expectations of them. I remembered Dr. Simons, Chris Ford, Ms. Gladney, Mr. Grosse, Ms. Geidt, Ed, and then Fedderly and Mr. P and everyone who had ever pushed me to be better. They never hesitated. They knew where the bar was and they told me to meet it—and every time I did, they set the bar higher.

Antonio sat down and played the étude I had assigned on his euphonium.

"You're doing this," I said, and picked up my tuba and played, *Do Bee Do Bee Do*, just like him. "I need you to do this." And then I put the tuba to my lips once more and played, *Do Bee Do Bee Dooooooooooooo*.

It was very clear what he needed to do. I wanted my students to know how good they could be, how good I expected them to be.

During one lesson with Steven Needham, another one of my tuba students, after he played the assignment, I pulled out my PT-7 tuba and handed it to him. I let all my students play my instrument.

"I'm not gonna tell you your family has to go into debt. I'm not gonna tell you that you *need* this, but I'm gonna let you play it so that you understand what you're capable of on a professional tuba. It is like upgrading from a Camry to a Bentley."

"This is how you do it! I sound like the record now!" Steven cried out.

Usually if you're an undergraduate tuba player, you play contrabass tuba. I made them learn contrabass and bass tuba. C and F.

"I'm an education major, why do I have to play F tuba?"

"Why do you need to be any less than a performance major?" There wasn't a substandard. I didn't care if it took them four years or seven; I just expected them to be on the level.

I could see that Jordan was worrying over how long the degree was taking him, so I told him the same thing I told Dontae sitting in Ms. Gladney's class. "Guess what? When you get your degree, it is going to say the same thing as the person who graduated in four years."

Jordan laughed. "Oh my gosh, it really is going to say the same thing."

"Yeah. Now, your transcript is a different story, but your degree will say the same thing. You can finish."

There's a tradition here in New Mexico that you commute to school to save money on room and board. It is just something that everyone does, like having a firearm.

"Take out a loan."

Their response was intense. "No, no, no, no, no, no, no, no. That's crazy, man. No way."

I suggested to Jordan that if he took out a loan, he'd be able to finish his degree sooner. "Do you want me to tell you how much debt I've got?" I had thousands and thousands of dollars in student loans.

"If you work forty hours a week and you're trying to go to school for eighteen credits, you being here for seven years is not totally your fault. You have to set up a system where you are allowed to achieve."

Jordan was like, "So what are you saying?"

"Work ten hours a week, man. Take out enough loans so that you can go to school. I'm not going to tell you to go into debt. But my philosophy is that your school is worth one year of tuition. So, you're in-state. If tuition costs ten thousand, you should have a maximum ten thousand for all four, six, or seven years of your school. You should pay for one year."

"That kind of makes sense."

"You do the math. You get a teaching job, you're making forty thousand, around three thousand a month. If you're making that, you can pay back ten thousand. You can do this, man. Don't give up."

"Yeah, but you know, it is hard on my parents."

"How proud would you be to say that you're a music teacher?"

"Tremendously."

"Graduating could change the whole trajectory of your family."

We sat there for a minute. I could hear the low notes of someone practicing tuba around the corner.

Then Jordan sat up and said, "I'm gonna finish."

Antonio was a little more mild-mannered. He flat out said, "I'm tired." He was working several jobs, commuting to school, and helping out at home.

"Guess what, you only have to get one job."

"What?"

"If you graduate and apply for all these jobs, you only have to win one."

"Oh yeah, I could do that." That's what I thought when Fedderly told me about winning an orchestra job.

"And then when you win one, we're the same. I've only won one more job than you."

There was a spark and Antonio gave me this look, like, *I'm gonna catch you.*

There was no tuba culture at UNM. There was no tuba culture in the entire state. There wasn't even a chapter of the International Tuba Euphonium Association (ITEA) in New Mexico. Mr. Phillips was adamant about fellowship and the ITEA was his brainchild. He held the first meeting in May 1973, the same month and year in which I was born.

We formed a chapter of ITEA and I named it after Mr. Phillips. Antonio did the paperwork and Jordan took a leadership role in the marching band. I gave them responsibilities and official titles they could put on their résumés. President of ITEA, which Jordan was. Vice president, which Antonio was.

All six of my tuba and euphonium students crammed into my tuba studio closet. This was a critical meeting. We had to forge a tuba culture. First item on the agenda: donuts.

When I told them we were going to have a donut stand, the entire studio groaned.

Jordan spoke up. "We don't sell donuts. This is not a moneymaker. This is so stupid."

"Well, if we don't sell donuts, we can't bring guest artists in."

"Why would we bring guest artists in?"

"Because you need to hear what your instrument can do."

Everyone was quiet.

"So," I said, "there are two goals to selling donuts. The first goal is for us to raise money and bring in guest artists. The second goal is, I want us to be the most notable organization on campus next to the football and basketball players."

We set up a donut stand manned by my six students and me. The kids decided to make a banner themselves: THE DONUT CORNER. Kids bought donuts. Teachers bought donuts. The dean of the fine arts department dropped twenty bucks into the donation bucket.

The donuts were just the beginning.

Back in Indiana, Mr. Phillips had told me about how he called Rockefeller Center and said, *I want to do Tuba Christmas.* Their response was, *No. Who the hell are you?* He said, *Well, I wish you would reconsider. Let me give you some of my references.* He gave them a list of who's who of music. The first person he gave them was Leonard Bernstein. Then he said, *You can call them and then I'll call you back tomorrow.* When he called back the next day, they had changed their tune. *Mr. Phillips, you can have whatever you want.* A new Christmas tradition was begun. Mr. Phillips had also started a fall celebration of the tuba, Octubafest.

Our first year, we started out small with Tuba Day. The theme the students picked was video games: The kids dress up in costumes and we play whatever the theme music is. Student services donated money to us, so we would always go play Christmas carols for them on Tuba Christmas. We also did something called ArtsMedicine, where we dressed in Santa suits and went to the hospital and played for the kids there. The staff loved it. The kids loved it too, and they called out requests, but Jordan and Antonio were bummed because we got many requests for songs that we didn't know. So we started expanding our palette of music so that the next year, we were ready.

For Tuba Valentine, we took a whole bunch of love songs from Motown and the pop charts and we sold TubaGrams. A tuba player would show up wherever your significant other was and play the song you requested.

We popped up all over campus playing love songs. I found one young woman in the cafeteria and started playing "My Girl." The whole lunchroom crowded around us. When I finished, they clapped and hooted and started calling out requests.

I smiled. "You gotta buy a TubaGram."

After that my students got a taste for the tuba antics and started coming up with their own ideas. They took it upon themselves to create a quartet called Euphoria. They went down to city hall and got a busking license and would perform downtown outside Popejoy Hall before every Broadway show, and they would play Christmas carols at the malls and made serious money.

The second year, I had twelve students and Octubafest was a weeklong affair. We had concerts where the community came, retirement homes came, the music appreciation class came, and that year when the chair came by the donut table and dropped twenty bucks in the bucket, he said, "You guys are doing amazing things. This is awesome."

My kids felt proud and so did I.

In the spring of my second year, Jordan poked his head into my office.

"Not only am I graduating, I already have a job!"

We were laughing and crying and then Jordan wrapped me in a giant hug.

29

Fearless and Inventive

Mr. Tux sold used tuxedos. I had always rented a tuxedo. It had seemed crazy to spend hundreds of dollars on something I'd wear in concert a few times a year. But now I had a job with the New Mexico Symphony Orchestra, and I had to wear a tux several times a week. The tailor measured and pinned.

When I stepped into my new tuxedo, the fabric was smooth and sharp. I didn't feel too big or too small, it was like stepping into my own skin, and for a second I imagined myself walking onstage carrying my tuba wearing the sleek black suit. I felt brand-new.

I owned everything I needed to do this work. I owned both my tubas, a tuba mute, all my cases, all my music. I was a professional!

We were preparing for a family concert of *Star Wars* and I would be playing the Jabba the Hutt solo. It is an incredible piece of music, all strings and tuba. It is high. It is rhythmically difficult. This was my first solo with the New Mexico Symphony Orchestra and I wanted to play it perfectly. I was untenured, so there was a lot of pressure; I couldn't afford to mess up.

I got the sheet music way in advance and started practicing. I'd record myself as I played, then I'd sit in my bedroom listening to the recordings and making notes in a journal. I studied myself. When I heard a recording of Gene Pokorny, principal tubist of the Chicago Symphony, playing, I thought, *That's how I want to play it*, and I listened to it on repeat for months.

By the time we began rehearsing, I was on point. Byron Herrington, who'd been on my auditioning committee, was conducting the show. Byron is one of the most gifted musicians and teachers I know. He is a trombonist, he plays jazz, he plays classical, and he conducts. In our last rehearsal, Byron said, "You're killing it, Richard." I glowed.

The day of our first performance, my nerves jangled. I went to the gym and ran on the treadmill, the music soaring through my brain as the machine thunked away beneath me. Then I did a scramble: shoulders, legs, chest, and sit-ups no matter what. Afterward, I went down to Popejoy Hall to warm up on both my F and CC tubas, which is cross-training. After practice, I lugged both tubas in from the car, and lay down to sleep.

I woke up, my body thrumming with excitement. I slipped into my black tux, laid both my tubas in my car, and drove to the adobe rectangles of Popejoy Hall.

Everything slowed down. I walked slowly. I sat slowly. I talked slowly, making sure that I was not out of breath. I buzzed into my mouthpiece and then walked onstage with both my tubas. There were a few people in the orchestra seated, flipping through their music, playing phrases on their instruments. I stared out at the sea of bright red seats and watched the audience stream in.

The concert hall was crowded with Luke Skywalkers and Princess Leias and Han Solos and Chewbaccas and Ewoks. There were grown-ups dressed as Stormtroopers and little kids running around as Darth Vader. Lightsabers *swoosh*ed through the air. The audience was bubbling in their seats, filling the hall with their excitement and joy; it was a wave I could ride.

I took a long, deep breath and just for a moment, allowed myself to think I had made it.

Three minutes before the show, there were still a few orchestral players missing. Jon Dante always walked in two minutes before the down beat, ready to play. He is an extraordinary trumpet player. Playing with him, I knew I had better bring it because you knew he would call you out. The orchestra reached new heights because he spoke his mind. He would erupt in rehearsal: "Are you serious? You guys need to practice. Are we going to play it like this? This is unacceptable."

Most of the time he nailed whatever he played but when he didn't, he went for it with such authority that you didn't mind if he missed, and he was always striving to be better.

We had played a Bach piece in a quintet and Jon was playing in a certain way—and not necessarily a good way—and he looked at me with those icy blue eyes and said, "Are you going to play like *that?*"

I stared at the tattoo snaking down beneath his ear.

"Yeah. I'm just copying you."

He looked at me with a snarl.

The next day he sounded amazing. He was nailing the phrase articulation. He looked at me and said, "Are you going to play it like me or what?"

The edge of my mouth twitched up into a small smile.

Waiting for Jon to come in and Byron to raise his baton, I closed my eyes and thought of the music and how I wanted it to sound. My stomach fluttered. I turned to Dave Tall sitting beside me holding his bass trombone—bass trombone and tuba are like Batman and Robin in an orchestra.

"Man, I hope I remember the fingerings."

"I hope so too." The bass trombonist chuckled.

The lights fell. The crowd hushed.

Byron raised his arms. Light glinted off his tiny wire-rimmed glasses. We all sat at attention and then dove into the *Star Wars* theme music. The hall went electric. Byron led us through "Luke and Leia" and "Parade of the Ewoks," and then we played "Jabba the Hutt." Strings and tuba. *Bee De Boo, Bee Dee Baaaw, Bee Dee Booo, Boo Baaw, Baaw, Baaw.*

Waiting to come in was like being at the top of a roller coaster—the dizzying height, my stomach dropping, the rush of air and music and fear and happiness.

Oh man. Don't breathe too much. Make sure you count. Watch Byron. Oh man, I hope I get the first high note. Okay, here we go. Weeeeee.

I was playing. *Oh, it's going well. Don't lose concentration. Don't pat yourself on the back. You need that hand to play the tuba.* The strings played high and I rolled through the music as it growled Jabba to life.

When I played the last low notes, the audience went wild. It was a total rumpus. I took a bow and sat down. The audience kept cheering and clapping and Byron directed me to stand again. I bowed low and sat back down, grateful.

After the show, Byron caught up to me and said, "You played the shit out of that."

The second night, Jon Dante said, "Awesome, man, even better than the first."

After the Sunday show, kids pointed at me, crying out, "Look, it's Jabba!" It was the closest to famous I'd ever felt.

I had played in other concerts here, of course, but playing Jabba was the first time I became the public's principal tuba player and not just the orchestra's. I felt heard.

30

A Visit with Midas

When I won the position with the New Mexico Symphony Orchestra, it was only a one-year contract. I thought New Mexico was a stepping-stone. Everyone around me told me I was going to get a big orchestra job in Boston or New York or some other big, glittering city. At first, I thought that's what I wanted. My predecessors had gone on to bigger and more prestigious orchestras. I would too. Only, I started to want to stay in New Mexico. I could imagine my whole life unfolding here. But people would call me and tell me about open spots or invite me to audition. I accepted invitations to audition in Pittsburgh and Milwaukee.

In Pittsburgh, when the cab I had called didn't show up to take me to the audition, the hotel offered me their limo. I stepped out of that black stretch thinking of Bill VerMeulen auditioning in his tux. I didn't advance.

After Pittsburgh, I knew something wasn't right and I needed to do my best at the Milwaukee audition. Orchestras all over the country were having financial trouble, but the Milwaukee orchestra was sponsored by Miller Lite and I figured Miller Lite was as stable an anchor as you could find. So I called David Fedderly and asked him to give me a lesson.

Fedderly is like Midas. He is the master of making you sound like you have a unique sound. Out of the last thirty jobs won by tubists, I'd hazard to guess that at least twenty of those people saw Fedderly before they took that audition.

I flew to Baltimore and went out to Catonsville, Maryland, where the Baltimore Brass Company, which Fedderly founded, has a warehouse. It is a low, gray, unassuming building with the name displayed in old-timey silver letters. I walked in and felt intimidated. My guard was up. Suddenly, I was aware that I wasn't a kid anymore: I was a man.

Fedderly hugged me, smiled, and ushered me into his office. I sat down to play and felt like I was eighteen again—green and uncertain.

Fedderly is old-school; he recorded me on a reel-to-reel and then let me hear the playback. In his soft voice, he said, "I want you to change a few things," and gave me a few notes. "I need you to breathe. I need you to relax." Then he pushed Record again.

I played. This time I felt the music open up ahead, me and my tuba coasting along. When I finished, Fedderly let me hear the two recordings back-to-back. The difference was astounding. In the second recording, you could hear the articulation of every note, you could hear the fullness of a phrase from beginning to end, and there was a softness, a delicacy that had been missing in the first recording. I was humbled.

The lesson progressed and I listened to everything he told me.

At the end I laughed and said, "Thank you." He had made playing fun again and had helped me find my voice.

Fedderly smiled, the little lines around his eyes gathered up. "You've improved a lot. Just remember, be you."

I flew to Milwaukee. When I got off the plane, my tubas were not there.

When I asked the man in the lost baggage office, he flatly said, "We have no idea where they are."

"What do you mean you have no idea?! Before I left Albuquerque, I watched the person at the desk put stickers on my two hard cases."

"We can't track where things are."

They had lost thousands of dollars in instruments and lost me the chance at a major job, and they didn't even know where these big, heavy, hard cases had got to? I was incensed.

I called the airline company. "I will sue you. I'm here to win a sixty-thousand-dollar job and you've lost my instruments! You can't do this."

The Milwaukee Symphony Orchestra agreed that if I got my tubas, they would hear me the next day before the second round began. The tubas arrived. The airline had them delivered to my hotel that night, and the next morning I played the preliminary round and I advanced. *Fedderly's Midas touch.*

After the second round, I was sitting in the green room listening to one of the other candidates play the Vaughan Williams tuba concerto. I was mesmerized. I had never heard it sound like that. When someone is really good, they can make a piece of music that we have all played a hundred times sound totally new and alive.

I could sound like that if I practiced a whole lot more, I thought to myself, and the whole room busted out laughing. I'd said it out loud.

"That's Carol Jantsch," someone told me. At twenty-one she had won the principal tubist position in the Philadelphia Orchestra and was the first woman to hold the spot of principal tuba in a major orchestra. She kicked my ass.

"You're never going to find the perfect job," Fedderly told me. "You find a job that you like and you turn it into a job that you love."

I went home to Albuquerque and decided that I really wanted to stay in New Mexico. I'd never been in a place with so much untapped potential; it was on its way to greatness. I wanted to witness that growth, to be part of it. I loved the big stretches of sky and the mountains that hold everything in perspective. I loved working for the NMSO and I loved teaching. This was where I wanted to be. Inspired by Mr. Phillips, I had fantasies about building a tuba ranch in the desert where people could come for a respite.

At the end of the first year, Abe Lillard, the orchestra's personnel manager, asked me, "Would you like to stay a second year?" I played the second year and then a third year. At the end of the third year, Steve

Campbell, whom I replaced, had won a tenured position at the Minnesota Orchestra and would officially be leaving the NMSO. Management was debating whether they should have a second national audition or give me tenure.

I got nervous. I thought they were going to have another national audition and I did not want to go through that again. If I had to, I might as well try for another orchestra. I told everyone who asked that I wouldn't take the audition.

The brass players rallied around me. Byron and Jon and Dave and Debra and Peter. They wanted me to stay. They talked to management. They talked to the other players. They pushed to have a vote on whether to offer me tenure.

The orchestra held a vote. It was unanimous. I belonged.

31

Rooted

I bought a house in Albuquerque. It was mine. I had a home of my own. I owned a piece of America. No more streets. I put down roots. Baltimore seemed incredibly far away and I knew that I wouldn't go back.

I called Mom and Dad all the time. We'd catch each other up and then, instead of saying I love you, I'd joke, "Maaa, I look good, don't I? My hair is longer than your husband's."

"Get out of here, boy," she'd tease.

I imagined life would keep flowing, that I would scrape together enough money to build a tuba ranch of my own. Harvey Phillips had inspired me. I wanted to create a sanctuary for people where they could come and, for a short while, the world would stop and they could play tuba and eat ramen. I wanted to offer people the respite I had found in so many places. It would stretch out in the New Mexico desert and have a stage and a giant sign that would read RAW TUBA RANCH in bright letters against the big open sky.

The collapse happened gradually. It was 2009 and the whole country was having financial troubles; the orchestra was just trying to survive. First, management took away our benefits—no healthcare, no pension. The next year, the problems with our paychecks began. At first, I got half of my paycheck and the management made an announcement that they would pay us the other half a little late, which they did. Then our paychecks shrank, and then they stopped coming altogether. Pretty soon, we weren't being paid at all. But everyone kept going to work. We showed up for every rehearsal. We played every concert.

One evening, almost the whole orchestra crowded into Linda's house. Linda was a violinist who lived close to Popejoy Hall. There were people leaning against the wall, balanced on armrests, and strewn across the floor.

We were all struggling with rent or mortgage payments, car notes, and forget about student loans. We were in dire straits. There were parents who couldn't pay tuition for their kids' school. Joe was hiding his car blocks from his house because he'd missed so many payments, he was afraid it would be repossessed. People who had an extra room or a second car offered them up to the other musicians. I offered my second bedroom to anyone who needed it.

"Hopefully some donor will come through," an old-timer said. That had happened before, in the '80s, when the NMSO had financial trouble.

Carla Lehmeier-Tatum stood up. She was the head of our Regional Orchestra Players Association, or ROPA, and she made sure everyone was registered with the union, which offered a relief fund, and explained how to collect unemployment.

I was still working as an adjunct professor at the University of New Mexico, making far from enough money to live on, but more than enough to disqualify me from collecting unemployment. Soon I burned through all my savings, and what I earned at UNM wasn't enough to cover my mortgage or pay utilities and medical bills, and I still had to eat.

I rotated bills. *I'll pay this one this month, and let that one slide for thirty days,* I'd tell myself as I riffled through the stack of bills at my kitchen table. Just checking the mail could make my stomach turn. I'd put a little down on this loan and hope that that would keep the dogs at bay.

It was an elaborate shell game. We were all waiting. We all thought the orchestra would right itself. When that didn't happen, we all thought the orchestra might close, but that a settlement would come through and we'd at least receive our back pay.

Everyone was just hanging on, but we kept playing and most of the orchestra wanted to wait it out. We would not strike.

After a year of working without pay, I had burned through any optimism. We couldn't just wait. We had to act. At one of our meetings, I spoke up. "This is insane. I don't see us getting paid." Someone told me to stay calm. Others nodded in agreement but were too scared to *do* anything.

"Well, what are we going to do?" Lori Lovato, a clarinetist, asked.

"We have to save the infrastructure. If we collapse this and start over, it will be years. It isn't going to come back in my lifetime," Dave Tall said.

There were older players who would be retired before the orchestra could resemble what they were leaving, and they were holding out hope that there'd be a turnaround. "We've been here before. The donors always come through."

"That's insane. You've been through this before and you think this is acceptable?"

"It will work out."

I shook my head.

Carla Lehmeier-Tatum and I became friends when I was elected to the negotiation committee after I received tenure. Carla was our union person and she knew all the rules, understood negotiation, and had an incredible gift for organizing and galvanizing the musicians. I'm a good talker. I opened up my mouth one day when I was frustrated and said, "I've never been in a place with so much potential that doesn't achieve it." All of a sudden, I was on the committee.

My first year on the negotiation committee, we got a really favorable contract. Days off, paid vacation, and if you didn't take the insurance, they paid you the premium. But once the financial trouble started, negotiations dragged on for months. Then they stalled. Then management presented their best, last, and final offer. An offer that would have put the musicians below the poverty line. We rejected it and they locked us out.

Management told the press that we refused to work. They tried to make it look like we had gone on strike, but we never went on strike. We wanted to play. Everyone in the orchestra loved their instrument, everyone loved music, everyone wanted to play. We shared a dream. A dream most of us had harbored since we were children, and management was trying to take that away.

I wanted to play. Ever since I'd picked up that trumpet in fourth grade, I had wanted to play, and whenever anyone had told me I couldn't or that I wasn't good enough, I had found a way.

32

Going to the Mattresses

I got by with way more than a little help from my friends, especially my brothers from Indiana.

"You need brakes on your car, man? I'm sending you the money. Don't worry about it. Whatever you need you got it, we'll keep a tab," Quincy told me. He'd graduated from the voice department and went on to own one of the biggest trucking companies in Dallas.

Larry, with whom I had pledged Kappa Alpha Psi, stood by me too. He and I used to be young and broke together. We would search our cars for change so we could get 99-cent Whoppers. Once I got the job at Indiana State and started playing with the Indianapolis Symphony, I was the one with money to spend. When he went to buy an engagement ring, I put it on my American Express. If he needed to travel to an opera competition, I put it on my American Express. He became a major opera star and when I ran into trouble he just said, "Where do you want me to send it?" Sometimes he'd give me a little flack. "Is this going on your tab too?" But he never made me feel small and he always let me know I was supported. If I actually tallied up what I owe Larry, it would be fifteen or twenty thousand dollars.

I even had to call my little brother, William.

"Yo, can you lend me fifty dollars? I'm waiting for a paycheck from a gig I did, but I gotta pay the water bill."

He was stunned and his voice went all soft. "Man, if you asking for this, you must really need this."

"Look, I promise I'll give this right back as soon as I get paid."

He sent me the money.

A few days later when my check came, I sent him back the money with interest. He called me up. "I can't believe you did what you said you was going to do."

I was confused. "What do you mean?"

"You asked me for money. I was sure that I wasn't going to get it back."

"But that's what we agreed to," I said.

"I know. But this happens all the time. A brother asks me for money and when I give it to him, I pretty much know I'm never gonna see that cash again."

I could pay fifty dollars back. But I didn't have the tens of thousands of dollars that I owed on my credit card bill, on my house, on my student loans. Every month I fell further behind on those payments. I'd even stopped opening the envelopes that were coming from Sallie Mae.

I pushed the screen door open and shuffled through the mail. The Capital One bill was $22,000 and I had graduated with six-figure student loan debt. There was something from Sallie Mae. *Trash.* There was a gas bill. *I paid that last month. Trash.* The electric bill hadn't been paid in a minute, so I tucked it and the mortgage statement under my chin and shoved everything else in the recycling.

The phone rang. I dug in my pocket and dropped the pile of mail to the floor.

"Hi, Dad. Everything okay?" I stared at the mess of paper.

"Boy, you need to tell me what's going on." Dad was shook.

"What are you talking about?"

"I got a call from some bill collector trying to get me to pay one of your loans to the tune of twenty-two thousand dollars."

"What are you talking about?"

"Some man called up the house and said that you owed twenty-two thousand dollars and that if I didn't clear your debt, they were going to take our house. Now, you gonna tell me what's going on?"

My brain was on fire.

It had cost me so much to get to this point in my career. I saw the price of it every month as I watched my loans balloon while I worked for an orchestra that wouldn't pay me, couldn't pay me. Now, to have some slimy creditor prey on my parents—it was too much.

I set up a three-way call with the collector and Dad.

I jumped in ablaze. "Hey, you don't call my parents. That's illegal. You don't have the right to do this. You knowing his credit card information is *bouillon*"—another of Dad's noncuss words—"and I know that it's a crime. So I am going to pay you what I can whenever I can and that is going to be the end of this. We can make a payment arrangement or deferment."

The collector knew he'd been busted and stayed quiet.

After the call, Dad was real easy. He said, "All right, you're going to take care of it. I got you covered." And that was that.

But my relationship with Ricky Jr. was strained. The truth is, it had been since the twenty dollars had gone missing when he stayed with me at Peabody. But after the collectors began calling my parents, Ricky Jr. started saying that I had a hundred thousand dollars of debt. He would tell anyone who would listen, "He went to school and my parents had to pay all his debt and now they're broke, this don't make no damn sense." It was all lies but it got under my skin. I burned with shame.

I called all the loan people—the banks, Sallie Mae, the collectors—and explained my situation. I told them how the orchestra went bankrupt and they wanted to know how I went bankrupt, and then I'd have to explain the whole thing again. Even to myself, I sounded crazy. I was working for free and hoping that the company would start paying me even though they had no money and hadn't been paying me for almost a year. The lenders weren't sympathetic. I'd have a gig here and there, I'd pay half the car note and a little bit on my credit card, and I borrowed more money from my friends.

By early 2011, my savings were gone and I was behind on the mortgage. I was too ashamed to call Quincy or Larry. William didn't have it and I would never ask my parents for money. I swallowed my pride and called Weston. He plays at the Metropolitan Opera in New York. I was pretty sure he'd be able to help.

"Look, man, you know, they're going to take my house if I don't fig-ure this out. I need seventeen hundred bucks."

"All right, Richard," he said heavily, "but what's the plan to pay me back?"

"Yo, I'll pay you back."

"Well, I know you wouldn't ask for it unless you really needed it."

I desperately needed it. Negotiations with management had come to a complete standstill. The lockout stretched on for months. The Play-ers Association, the PA, kept meeting in people's homes, we leafleted neighborhoods, we got donations from fans, we got donations from big donors, we got donations from other orchestras in other cities.

We crowded into Linda's living room again.

Denise Reig Turner stood up and we quieted down. We'd raised enough money that it would help all us musicians pay off our bills. "We need to decide if we are going to distribute this money among the musi-cians or put it into the PA toward our future."

"All in favor of distributing the funds among the musicians?"

I kept my hand down at my side and glanced around. Not a single person had raised their hand.

"All in favor of saving it for the future of the orchestra?"

All of our hands rose.

We planned our first community concerts ourselves. We didn't have money to rent sheet music, so we borrowed some from UNM and the per-formance was held in an old church in downtown Albuquerque. When I walked into the chancel, I looked out at the sea of people. The wooden pews were filled, the aisles were crowded. People were pouring out the doors into the courtyard where speakers were set up.

The music rolled through the church, lifting everyone with it. I closed my eyes and let it roll through me. I imagined it pulsing out into the New Mexico night sky. Rolling across the desert and up to the stars.

I opened my eyes and saw the audience and my colleagues and I knew we were doing what we were supposed to do.

But by the third community concert, I couldn't help but think that really, I was just doing the same thing I had been doing for management—I was working, but I wasn't getting paid. Most of the orchestra was still holding out hope that the NMSO would somehow come back, but it looked like a sinking ship to me. I was going to have to begin auditioning again, and my stomach roiled.

Everyone at the University of New Mexico knew what was happening at the orchestra. As we sat in the music office, I told Steve Block, the chair, that I was going to have to start looking for a new job. He told me, "Well, we want you to stay. We would love to give you a position. We just don't have the money." That seemed to be the running theme.

I had been teaching adjunct the whole time I'd been at the school and that wasn't enough money. I needed a tenure-track, full-time job.

"So, if I find the money, you'll give me a tenure-track position?"

"Yes. That's what I'm saying."

It would have been easier to just walk away and start over somewhere else. In a bigger, more deeply funded orchestra. But I resisted the thought of leaving. That old hardness inside me sparked: *I am here. I am not going anywhere.* I didn't like the audition process, but more than that, I had Harvey Phillips in my head. I hadn't done everything I could do in this state yet.

There were a handful of us who were opposed to just carrying on in the same way. Lori, Denise, Carla, and Terry Pruitt, a bass player.

We were sitting around backstage at the church after rehearsal one day when Terry confided in me. "I'm going to file a labor complaint."

"What are you doing exactly?" This was the first time anyone had told me that they were doing anything other than what the group was doing. Curiosity crashed through my brain.

"Look," Terry said, "the NMSO is going to go bankrupt and if you are not on a complaint list you aren't going to get paid."

"Really?" I had no doubt the NMSO was going under, but I had trusted that at some point we'd be paid what we were owed and I could pay off my debt.

"If this all goes down tomorrow and the orchestra files for bankruptcy," Lori explained, "then the lawyers are going to get paid, all the debtors are going to get paid, and then the musicians are going to get paid according to the order they filed in."

Lori, Terry, and Denise had been with the orchestra since the '90s. Their lives were in Albuquerque. They didn't want to pick up and start over somewhere new. They gave me a copy of the paperwork to file a labor dispute complaint and the name of a lawyer.

I sat at my kitchen table that night and filled it out, and the next morning I met with the lawyer and we filed an unfair labor practice claim against the New Mexico Symphony Orchestra.

That's when the shit hit the fan.

"Can you explain to me why you did this, Richard?" Kevin Hoggins, the board president, asked.

"Because where I'm from, you work, you get paid. It's simple."

"We can't have a run on the bank if all these people file complaints," another board member screamed at me later that day in front of some of the orchestra members. Panic was making his voice shrill. I just listened. "What's preventing the whole orchestra from doing this?"

"Nothing," I said flatly, and hung up.

An hour later the same board member called me back.

"Richard, if you drop your complaint, we'll file Chapter 11 instead of Chapter 7." Chapter 11 meant that they would reorganize their debt but keep operating. Chapter 7 meant the orchestra was done.

I called my lawyer and dropped the complaint.

Then the board member called a meeting. The orchestra was there, the management was there, the lawyers were *all* there. But he didn't announce that they were filing Chapter 11. Instead, he said that they would file Chapter 7 and we would forgo any back pay and would keep working as usual.

Fury pulsed through me. "Why would I do that? Services have already been rendered. This would be a different conversation if you had come to me before I worked for a year with the understanding that I would be paid." We were not talking about $10,000, we were talking about $42,000.

"We can't take a chance on there being a run on the bank. We're filing Chapter 7."

I reopened my complaint and Kevin told all the other players that I had brought the orchestra to its knees. It stung but there wasn't time to worry about being excommunicated. If the NMSO was filing Chapter 7 we had to do something fast if we were going to keep an orchestra in Albuquerque.

33

Invent the Future

Carla and I sat at my wooden kitchen table. The sun was falling and we had a pot of coffee and a bottle of wine.

She had called her ROPA counterpart in Colorado Springs. They had just gone through the same thing. They advised us to take advantage of the bankruptcy filing to buy everything we could—the library of music, the chairs, the stands, any piece of equipment we would need. We also had to have a board. Carla and I worked our way down the list of names we'd compiled: major funders, a lawyer, a banker, a list of professionals across the community. We told them that we were going to build an orchestra ourselves. *Would you like to join our board?*

Everyone said, *Absolutely.*

So we sat at my kitchen table and put the paperwork together for a new 501(c)(3).

"What should we be called?" Carla asked me, drumming her fingers on the table.

"We should be called the NM Phil."

"Why?"

"Because people might mistake us for NY Phil, or anybody that's Phil that's actually getting paid right now."

Carla snorted a laugh.

We filed paperwork for the New Mexico Philharmonic. As soon as the NMSO filed for Chapter 7, we put in a bid to buy the library. The orchestra association voted to use our funds and we bought the equipment, scores to symphonies and concertos, and all the sheet music for the individual parts. We saved thousands of dollars—by the time the NMSO officially closed, we had enough in place so that we started as a two-million-dollar orchestra.

I still didn't have a paycheck, but I had an orchestra.

My phone rang and I hesitated, expecting an unidentified number with a creditor behind it. But my screen lit up with Mr. P's name. "Hey, Mr. P," I said, my voice bouncing up with relief.

He asked me how I was doing, and then he dove right in. "Look, I'm calling because your degree is going to expire. You really need to finish this degree."

"Okay, I will," I said, imagining the paperwork I had to fill out for another extension.

"No, it expires tomorrow."

"Are you kidding me?"

I called Indiana University the next day and they granted me an extension. They also told me that I had to pay my back tuition, which was $21,000.

I thought I was going to be sick. I forced air in and out, in and out.

"Okay," I said to the lady on the phone in the bursar's office, "That's not gonna happen. I don't have this kind of money. What do I do?"

They gave me a few weeks to get it together. But before we got off the phone, she warned me: "There's nothing more we can do for you before your degree is forfeited."

I couldn't call Larry or Weston or Quincy. I owed so many people so much money. But I was desperate, so I swallowed my pride and thought of our new board members and who might be willing to help.

I ran to my desk. I had a list of five board members I thought *might* help.

I dialed the first number on my list and the magical person on the other end said, "Richard, I'm happy to help. Good luck." Magical person gave me a $4,500 check.

My second call was to Susie Pool, who had been the first female opera student at Curtis. When I explained my predicament, she said, "Richard, this is worth it," and offered to pay the rest of the tuition.

Gratitude radiated through me.

I got the revised proposal in a few weeks later and finished the rest of the process and my dissertation in a few months. Then I waited for approval.

I still hadn't received approval in May 2012 when I arrived in Indiana for my graduation ceremony. I was seated beside the Dean of Graduate Academics. The announcer was reading off the "S" names when my phone vibrated. It was a text saying my dissertation had been approved. *Congratulations.* I flashed my phone at the dean, who said, "Only you, Richard. Perfect timing."

Then the announcer called my name, presented me with a leather folder for a diploma, and declared me Dr. Richard Antoine White.

William was the first person I called.

"Man, you're the first Black man to get a doctorate of music in tuba. Wow. Congrats."

But when I opened the leather holder, there was no diploma.

I went to the office to find out where my diploma was and they presented me with a bill for eighteen hundred dollars.

"What is this for?" I asked, incensed.

"Oh, computer fees, transportation, and so on."

"I wasn't even on your campus to need transportation. I didn't use your computers. What kind of racket is this?" I was indignant, and I was also still broke. Though we had filed paperwork for the New Mexico Philharmonic, nobody was taking home a paycheck yet.

Still, I was Dr. Richard Antoine White.

I had a doctorate and I had helped establish a new orchestra, but I still didn't have a full-time gig and it would be years before the Philharmonic would be able to pay full salaries. I needed a tenure-track job at the University of New Mexico. I started talking to Finnie Coleman in the African American studies department, but while they were very supportive of me and my work, they didn't have any money. I went home that night and asked myself: *Who has the most money on campus?*

The football team.

Then I thought, *Well, what can I offer the football team?*

Hey, man. They gotta know how to breathe.

The next day, I called up the athletic director and said, "Hey, can we have a meeting? I can teach your athletes respiratory functions." (I tried to keep it academic.)

He loved the idea and asked me to be the assistant marching band director too. The band was pretty important. We had one of the weakest football teams in the division. No one was coming to the games to watch football.

The athletic director asked me if I could get fifteen tubas.

"In my sleep."

Then I went back to my closet of a tuba studio and called a student meeting.

"Hey, I need a favor. I need all of you to sign up for marching band."

They did.

The football team supplemented the rest of my salary, and so I became a full-time, tenure-tracked professor. UNM still had the worst football team in the country, but at least *we* were entertaining.

My graduate student Paul Carlson drove us to Santa Fe one night. It was a long brown road and the sky was full of lightning as we passed reservations and casinos. Paul and I had met when we'd arrived at UNM. He was studying with another tuba professor but wanted to take lessons with me, so I taught him on the side for free and we grew close. He was like a younger brother. We were driving down to Santa Fe to see Dontae Winslow play at the Lensic Theater.

When I was still in Indiana, Dontae had called me up when he got into the Thelonious Monk Institute of Jazz at the University of Southern California. After high school, he went to a music program in New York and then transferred to Peabody after I left, to join their jazz program. He was teaching in Baltimore public schools.

"Yo, I got a wife and a baby. I'm teaching and I'm making good money. I don't know if I should go."

"What do you want in life?"

"I want to be a star."

There was only one answer. "Then you gotta move." He didn't say anything, so I kept talking. "You ain't gonna be a star in Baltimore. If you want to be a star, move to LA. Go to where the stars are."

You must take chances. If you don't, you can be assured of one thing: You definitely won't win.

Dontae took the chance. He quit his teaching job and moved to LA with no idea how he was going to make ends meet. Once, he called me up pretty stressed. "Yo, I don't know what to do, the mortgage is due." That month I didn't pay my mortgage and sent him a thousand.

Being in Santa Fe watching Dontae was astonishing. He was up onstage playing this black flügelhorn, which looked amazing, and he sounded *ridiculous*. We'd come a long way since picking up our trumpets in fourth grade. I was so proud of him and he was proud of me too. I'd talked to him after I finally got the doctorate, and he'd made me feel uncomfortable with the way he'd raise me up. We'd be talking about work and all of a sudden he'd say, "Man, a Black man, first doctorate in tuba, principal tubist of the New Mexico Symphony Orchestra. Yo, this is history, man. Look at you, man."

"Come on, man," I said, embarrassed.

Every now and then he'd call to talk about technique and it would always end in him saying something ridiculously hyperbolic.

Dontae asked me, "How do you hit the high notes?"

I gave him a warm-up routine and after he used it, he said, "Man, you a genius. All these years nobody ever told me this. I mean, the high notes, Justin Timberlake, it's not even hard, man. Tell me about the warm-up, man. Send me a video of you using the warm-up."

Once I told him, "The air must never stop. The tongue must assist the air."

He said, "Yo, you gotta get that tongue out of the way. You're a genius. How am I gonna play trumpet all these years and no one ever told me this?"

In the same conversation, I told him something I noticed about his playing. "You favor the right side of the phrase. You've got to focus on the end. Save something to the end of the note. You always have to finish."

"That's the most useful thing I ever heard." He gave me way too much credit, of course. But that's Dontae. He and his wife call each other King and Queen. But I also understand the immense pride and self-belief he has in himself and promotes in the people he loves. We had come a long way from Lafayette Market and Cross Country Elementary, where we'd squeaked into our trumpets in the band room. We'd lost our moms, escaped violence, defied the odds in a thousand ways, and now we were both living our dreams, though maybe my orchestral work hadn't gone the way I had imagined.

The New Mexico Philharmonic's first performance was Mahler's Symphony No. 2—the *Resurrection* Symphony. We played it in Popejoy Hall. The march of the horns and the drums thrummed in my chest, and the strings floated delicately, raising us all up, higher and higher. The notes built stronger and stronger, triumphant and then easing into a whisper. The audience fell under Mahler's spell. The music roiled and danced, moving forward and carrying us along until the final notes. When Uriel Segal, our conductor, dropped his arms with a flourish, the hall filled with jubilation.

The audience were on their feet, roaring. I looked around at our orchestra—some of us were bawling, others laughing, sitting quietly, or rushing into one another's arms. We had been through the fire. Some players had retired. Some had left for other orchestras. One of our violinists had passed away. Our orchestra had been dismantled and yet, here we were, together, making beautiful music and sharing it with people.

Carla Lehmeier-Tatum and Derek DeVelder, who was a contra bass player in the NMSO at the time, came up to me as we were walking offstage and said, "Thank you."

A warmth spread through me.

This was where I belonged. This was my orchestra. This was the orchestra where I'd won my first full-time tuba job. This was the orchestra where I'd earned tenure. This was the orchestra that had raised me. This was the orchestra that had collapsed and that I had helped to resurrect.

34

Here, Now

"Your mom is gone, boy." Dad's voice was soft and sadder than I'd ever heard it.

"Oh no, Dad. I'll book a flight. I'm on my way."

Mom's health had been deteriorating since I had left for Indiana, and Dad had cared for her unfailingly. He did everything. He would pick her up out of the bed, place her in a hoist to help her use the bathroom, clean her up after, and then set her in the chair so she could sit up for a little while before he put her back in bed and tucked her in. He sat by her bed and read the Bible to her, cooked for her, and fed her.

In fact, she would not eat until Dad came home. If Dad had to go to church or to work and I said, "Ma, you want to eat?" she said, "No, just give me some water. I'll wait for your father."

Sharing a meal was their way of connecting.

When the doctors told Dad to put Mom in hospice, he resisted. Caring for her was the way he knew how to love her. That was a family trait—that was the way she had always loved me. Though sometimes that love was as tough as nails.

Once, when I was in junior high, I wanted to go hang out with my homies and Vivian told me no. Well, I wasn't going to take that. I thought I was old enough and that I could do whatever I wanted.

I made the mistake of telling her, "I'm leaving. I'm done."

She didn't miss a beat. "Great. Let me help you." And she went and got a trash bag and started packing my stuff.

"What are you doing? You're crazy."

"No. You're leaving. Let me help you leave." And she kept packing my stuff.

"I'm just playing."

"No. No. You weren't playing. You don't get to take it back. You're leaving. Good luck. Good luck paying rent. Good luck figuring out where you gonna stay. Let me put all your stuff in the bag," she said as she threw my shirts and shoes and underwear into big black trash bags. She paused. I thought she was done; she had made her point. Then she said, "Oh, actually, I bought this, this is not your stuff," and started taking everything back out. She gave me the bag and said, "Go on. Go."

I just sat on the edge of the bed, and she was like, "What's the matter?"

"I changed my mind."

I like to imagine her walking out of my room and telling the story to Dad, and the two of them laughing. She was always good at laughing. I would miss that too, joking with her.

I'd come home from Indiana and tell her about my exams and she'd wave me off and say, "Oh, you big old dummy."

"You know, Mom, school actually means I'm smart."

"You heard what I said," she'd say, a sly smile creeping across her face.

We both knew the truth—I was her baby. Even as a kid, if I wanted something, she would always get it for me. If I wanted twenty bucks, she'd tell my dad, "Give it to him." If he hesitated, or started to say anything, she'd jump right in, "I said give it to him."

She was the person who raised me and she was my best friend. You know things are right when no over-the-top praise is needed. You just know that it is right.

During these trips home, as Mom had it harder and harder, Dad and I got more time alone together and he probably talked to me more on those visits than he had my entire childhood.

I asked him how he knew Mom was the one he wanted to marry. "You know, man, I mean, she was just the prettiest one. And we could go places." And he told me something I had never thought about. "You know, she could go both sides up here. And nobody would question it." I had no idea what he meant. "What do you mean, both sides?"

He explained: "Because she was so light-skinned they didn't know. You know, she could go on both sides and she was so pretty."

She even looked pretty in the casket, which lay amid a sea of flowers— she always loved flowers—in front of the choir pew. Coming to the church, I'd been sad and scared. I remembered the way Mama's arm had been cold and hard when I touched it at her funeral years ago. But Mom's body didn't frighten me—instead, she looked at peace and I was relieved because she'd suffered for so long.

I was standing next to my dad when he took Mom's hand and fixed her ring. When he'd finished, he stood beside her for a long moment. His cheek was wet with tears and I put my hand on his back.

During the funeral, one of the deacons said a prayer and a few words. Then he stood and spoke, telling my dad, "Vivian may have been your wife, but she was my girlfriend." Soft laughter rose up around me. That same deacon had celebrated my parents' fiftieth wedding anniversary when they renewed their vows years ago.

Mom had looked real pretty. She had on a special wig and a purple dress. When she came out of their room, she was glowing. I knelt down to help her with her shoes. Her feet were swollen and I couldn't get the shoe on. I was trying to be gentle.

"No, put the shoe on, boy," she instructed.

I was afraid of hurting her.

"There's no way you can hurt that leg," she said. "I ain't got no feeling in it."

Dad came out in his suit. "Yeah, fifty years."

My dad doesn't have any electronics in the house, so he's an old-school, do-it-yourself Renaissance man. He built a ramp.

I started wheeling Mom and her heavy-ass motorized chair down the ramp, thinking, *Man, you must eat spinach and oatmeal every day.* I almost lost that wheelchair. I thought it was going to fly down the ramp, straight into the neighbor's house across the street.

"Oh, just push it on down there, boy. What's the problem?"

"What's the problem? This thing weighs a million tons."

"Oh, get out the way, boy." And then he just did it like there was nothing to it.

Everyone was at the church. All their church folk. All Mom's friends from the hospital and all Dad's buddies from years back when he owned a bar. Angie and Rhonda and Richie were there with all of Mom and Dad's grandkids sitting at the front of the church, but I was in the back with Mom, because I was walking her down the aisle.

We were waiting for everything to get started when, looking at my dad standing up front looking dapper, Mom leaned toward me and said in a loud whisper, "Uh-huh. They all want him, but I got him."

"No, you didn't!" I started laughing so hard I didn't know if I'd be able to stop by the time I had to walk her down the aisle.

Joe, the organist at their church, started playing, and he can *really* play. He can't read music, but he can play by ear like nobody's business. I did stop laughing, but I didn't even try to stop smiling as I walked my mom to the front of the church where my dad took her hand and bent down to kiss her.

The bigness of their love rolled out into the church, joy bouncing off every surface. I grinned and cried and thanked the universe for my family.

At the funeral, I was a pallbearer along with my cousin Antoine, Angie's son, and a couple of church members.

Holding the casket with Mom's body aloft, I began to cry. She had carried me so far, made sure I'd arrived safely, and now she was gone. My vision blurred, and I choked on a sob.

At the back of the church, I saw a single white face. As I drew closer,

David Fedderly came into focus. He leaned into the aisle and whispered, "Ya'll sure do things different." I just about dropped the casket. I bit my cheeks and tried not to laugh.

After the service, I found Fedderly milling about. He was easy to spot amid the Black and brown faces.

"I can't believe you're here," I said, embracing him.

"People were incredibly nice, but they kept asking if I was lost. And I just kept saying, I am a friend of Richard's." I smiled at the thought that he had tasted the medicine I'd been swallowing all these years.

We talked about my mom and Peabody and the BSO and Steven Needham, the student who had heard me play at a southwest tuba conference and transferred from Las Vegas to UNM to study as an undergraduate. I'd sent him to Fedderly to get his master's at Peabody. He was the first student I had sent over and I felt everything had come full circle.

Fedderly had seen me through so much death and joy. Seeing him now filled me with calm. In my head, I still heard the pure sound of his tuba in the Peabody atrium and thought of how far I had come since then. Since I'd met him at Baltimore School for the Arts, since I'd picked up that first trumpet, since I'd left Sandtown and made a home with Richard and Vivian.

I found Dad and hugged him. He patted me on my back. We didn't need to say anything more.

Mom's death reminded me to live with a sense of urgency. I don't believe I'm going to live long. I'm always scared. I always feel behind, because I think my time might be limited. Seems like the universe plays games like that—something good happens, then something bad happens. There's an awkward duality—up, down, left, right. Good, bad. In love. Out of love. I just try to do as much as I can as fast as I can.

The World Deserves
the Best Version of You

William called me in Albuquerque once. He was twisted up about something and he just laid it on me. "Yo, how come you never call? You never want to talk to me."

"Look, man, I don't know you. My family is my adopted family. I don't know your middle name. I don't know when you were born. How am I supposed to talk to someone I don't know?" I explained.

"Dang. I never thought about that."

We were quiet for a while. The cell was hot on my ear.

Finally, William said, "Well, we should work on this, man. Let's just start by checking in and making sure each other is okay."

After that conversation, we started talking, really talking. We checked in on each other. I would tell him about my life and he would tell me about his. He told me that I was the reason that he wanted to be off the streets and had gotten a job at Walmart. He wanted to make me proud, and he did.

I introduced him to classical music and it spoke to him, gave him calm, and it made me happy to share something I loved with him.

As we grew closer and he learned more about me and my life, he started defending me to the family. One day William reported, "I tell everyone that my brother really plays in the New Mexico Philharmonic and they don't even believe me."

"Really? Why would you make *that* up?" I laughed. But knowing that they felt that way stung. My heart ballooned, and I blurted out, "I love you." *That was a little weird*, I thought.

The folks left in Sandtown thought that I was some persnickety guy going to fancy schools and getting fancy jobs and forgetting where I came from. They were all wrong. I thought about where I came from every day. I carried Sandtown with me into every classroom, onto every stage. To my mom Cheryl's family, I didn't belong anymore, but here was William making me feel that I did. I belonged.

Years later, filmmakers David Larson and Darren Durlach started working on an idea for a short documentary about underfunding in the arts. On a recommendation from Chris Ford, they spoke to me, and their film about the arts turned into a documentary about my life.

When I dragged my trash bag into Richard's green Buick all those years ago, I packed those Sandtown memories away and moved on. Other than Mama, what was there for me to miss? So when we came back to Baltimore for the documentary, I was unprepared. Returning to Sandtown was like being hit by lightning. Only instead of being electrocuted, I was electrified, every emotion awakened. I'd turn a corner and a new memory would blossom, like I was growing up all over again. The past and future existed simultaneously.

The documentary had my old life in Sandtown and my tuba life bumping up against each other. When we started talking about the soundtrack, I mentioned that William could rap and they got really excited and asked me to bring him by the studio. *He'll do a little freestyle and we'll just work it out*, they said.

They are film people; they have no idea that music doesn't work like that. "Does the producer have some bass lines?" I asked.

"Oh, he'll give you something when you get to the studio."

"Well, does he have some themes, some stuff that he wants?" I pressed.

"Yeah. He's got some ideas. He wants some happy sounds, some serious sounds. You can do that, right? He'll explain it to you when you get to the studio," they said breezily.

"Excuse me, no practice?"

The day of our recording session, the producer Sean Mercer greeted me at the studio. Nerves gnawed at me. I was sweating and off-kilter. I didn't know what would happen with William. I didn't know if he would show up. I didn't know if he would be on time. I didn't know if he would be prepared. I didn't know his professional demeanor. I didn't know anything about doing a rap session either—I hadn't made any kind of rap music since Tupac conducted us in the cafeteria my freshman year of high school. I couldn't practice specifically for today because I didn't know what Sean wanted, and that made me uncomfortable too.

But at some point, you just get so scared that you're beyond being scared.

I sat down in front of the mic and picked up my tuba. The feel of the heavy brass in my hand was comforting. Sunlight flooded into the studio and Christmas lights glittered across the ceiling. The whole place glowed. I focused on my breathing.

"Yeah, man, I need Questlove with some Stravinsky and you know, *Rite of Spring.*"

Excuse me? Are you nuts? What century am I supposed to be in? What's happening here? My brain couldn't cross-reference it. But I brought the tuba to my mouth and out came music. *Shamp Shamp Shamp Shamp Shamp Shamp—oh, Stravinsky, Questlove. BAM.*

We kept working and Sean kept getting me to do all kinds of things that I hadn't done before, pushing my limits. Then William opened the door, right on time.

"What's up, kid?"

"What's up with you, man?"

I set my tuba down and pulled William in tight. I was nervous and excited and grateful.

The film people were trying to manipulate the situation a little bit, they would catch us talking and try to needle us to do a little freestyle right then for the camera. We were reluctant; we don't really do that. It isn't like we grew up together having impromptu music sessions all the time. We'd never made any kind of music together.

When William finished, I said, "Daaaammmn. All right, bro. We're going to do this today."

The atmosphere in the room loosened. William was a little embarrassed and nervous too, and as I sat down to finish recording, he went outside to smoke. When he came back in, he stepped into the sunny recording booth and stood behind the mic. He pulled his hands down over his eyes. I worried. Then he wiped the sweat off his face with his T-shirt and he was ready.

I asked Sean if he'd given William topics.

"Baltimore. Family," Sean said.

"And brothers. Us," I added.

"Beat drop," William said, and the beat we'd made with the tuba and trumpet came in and William began, his voice rough and rich and easy. "What's up, Richard / You got your brother on the track."

He flowed and the room cracked open. We were still quiet but I could feel each of us fall under his spell, hanging on his words. His gold chain caught the light as he rocked back and forth spitting a freestyle that made me laugh and shake my head in wonder. I stared at the red, white, and black knobs on the mixing table, listening closely, smiling hard enough that my cheeks hurt. I'm a classical musician but I know good music when I hear it—it doesn't matter if it is an aria or a rap.

I was amazed at what my little brother could do. At what we had done together. It was still a little hard to believe that we were even in this studio together. That we had both survived at all seemed like a minor miracle. But the evidence was humming through the speakers. Two brothers raised in one city but a world apart, connected by music.

William finished and the energy in the room exploded.

Dang.

"You spit like that, man!" He walked in from the recording booth and I pulled him in close. "That's Baltimore, man. That's Baltimore."

William played it cool, but I knew what we had just done.

"You know Mom is smiling at us, man."

We recorded a few more tracks and then took a walk. The street looked familiar, weeds pushing up through sidewalk cracks, boarded-up windows, squat brick buildings pressed against each other. We talked about everything—music, the moment when we first met, that conversation when we'd decided to really try to get to know each other, and Mama.

The last thing my mother told William when she was dying of an asthma attack was, "I want you to be like your brother." For her to say that with her last breath was proof that she loved me even though she had to give me up.

It took me years to see that my mama was a hero. She did one of the hardest things for any mom to do—she gave up her kid. She let me live with Vivian and Richard, Mom and Dad, so that I would have a better life. That is love.

She would have been so proud of William and me—proud of the music we are making, the lives we are living. I looked at my brother sitting beside me on the white marble steps outside one of the boarded-up buildings.

We are here, now. Anything is possible.

No one is born great. We may have certain advantages or disadvantages, but no matter what we have or what we lack, we must nurture our own greatness. We have to know our own dreams and do everything within our power to achieve them, and we must, above all, maintain hope.

Hope is a powerful driving force that can propel you toward what you want. I think of hope as having four pillars:

H for holding on
O for being an opportunist, being ready to take advantage of an opportu-
nity when one presents itself
P for persistence
E for excellence

This mnemonic helps me remember that I am my own force for change. Sometimes in life you have to be your own hero. You have to consistently raise yourself up, constantly push yourself to grow, and always strive for greatness. Auditioning for a job in an orchestra was a clarion call—being good wasn't enough. I had to grow great.

It turns out that my audition for the Baltimore School for the Arts was the easiest audition I ever had. It wasn't because I was great or because I'd practiced longer and harder than anyone—I hadn't. It was because Chris Ford and the entire school hold a profound belief in the potential of their students. They believe that opportunity can foster meaningful change. That school gave me more than an education, it gave me a chance to choose what my life would look like. A lot of people in my family and a lot of people in Sandtown never got chances like that.

Not too long ago, my aunt Regina told me, "The seventies was a wicked time. All of us was strung out on something. Everybody was fighting their own demons. Don't be mad at them." She said that everybody had problems—my aunts and uncles, the whole neighborhood. In Sandtown, and a whole lot of other places too, there were people suffering from addiction to alcohol and heroin. There were people struggling with poverty, mental illness, and a lack of opportunity in education and work. To be honest, it doesn't look that different now.

The McClains scooped me out of Sandtown and Baltimore School for the Arts gave me a chance to make choices that would change my life. It is up to all of us to preserve and protect the right for all our youth to have the ability to make good choices, good change, and a real difference—to themselves and their communities.

Some of those changes may be big, like sponsoring a scholarship or fostering a child, but they can also be as small as a Cup Noodles. During a talk I gave at a national convention for teachers, a man stood up and asked, "What happens when you reach a wall with a kid who you believe is reachable, but you can't get through to him?"

I didn't think about my answer, the words just tumbled out of my mouth. "Feed him."

The man stared at me with a confused look on his face.

"Keep Cup Noodles in the closet." Kids often come to school starving, and that makes focusing next to impossible.

A few weeks later, I received an email from the man asking, *How did you know that?*

People often hear my story and comment that I pulled myself up by my bootstraps. That's part of the American myth, after all. But we have to acknowledge that not everyone has boots and straps to pull. If you're hungry, you're going to have a much harder time sitting through class, learning, and excelling. If you don't excel, you risk being left behind. That teacher feeding a student Cup Noodles is taking the first step to give that kid a chance to make choices that will change his life. Change is possible.

When President Barack Obama was elected, I felt like real change was happening. For the first time, someone who looked like me was going to be president of the United States. Until then, the possibility of systemic change was theoretical; after his election, change became tangible.

After the documentary, *R.A.W. Tuba*, came out, I spoke at the Annie E. Casey Foundation in Baltimore, not far from where I'd been found during the blizzard. They'd asked me to speak to a group of at-risk kids.

I looked out at all those young faces. I knew they were living hard lives. I saw myself in them. As I told them about my life, I was overwhelmed by the kindness and imagination and big love that had saved me again and again. I had been saved by the doctors at Maryland

General Hospital; by my uncle Ricky Jr., who shot off the rats; by Vivian and Richard McClain, who took me in and became my family; by my mother, Cheryl, who let me go and loved me always; by all the people who taught me music, pushed me to be great, and made change possible.

"Take a deep breath." I inhaled and gestured for the kids to do the same. "Sit up straight." The whole audience rose up a few inches. "Now, repeat after me: I can change."

"I can change," they shouted.

"We can change."

"We can change," they shouted.

"My challenge to each of you today is to present change to the world by offering the world your absolute best. You can change. I can change. We can change. We shall change. We must change. Together, we will change."

By the end, we were all shouting together and I was electrified with hope. It is simple, I know. But each time I hear all those voices shouting out those words, I'm overwhelmed by the limitless potential in the room. I know what is possible.

I believe in the cumulative effect. I don't want to let the universe down and I don't want to deprive the world of the best version of me. That attitude is contagious. I believe each of us must become our own superheroes. I am made up of what I have control over: my thoughts, the images I visualize, and the actions I take. Imagination is not bullshit; it is our superpower. It is how we create change. No matter how hard the journey is, no matter how tiring it is, I won't stop. There is something beyond the point of exhaustion: a new beginning.

I have forged a new beginning in Albuquerque, New Mexico. I have a home. I have a family—Yvonne, the love of my life, and her three kids, Savonn, Samaira, and Raelynn, and our dog, Tulula. I belong.

My personal vision for change is to establish the RAW Tuba Ranch. It will be a place of fellowship, where anyone can come twenty-four hours a day to make music, eat chili or ramen, and have a cold beer. It will be a place where you belong. That's my happy-ever-after ending.

Acknowledgments

It takes a village. I've always believed that when things are uncertain or unsure, it's good practice to start every sentence as best you can with, "It's a fact." It's a fact the actual production of this book happened because of the following amazing people behind the scenes with their own extraordinary talents: Sarah Murphy, Lindsay Edgecombe, Alexis Gargagliano, Sydney Jeon, Christopher Smith, Jordan Forney, Keith Hayes, Zack Wagman, Bob Miller, and everyone at Flatiron Books! I am forever grateful for your expertise and dedication toward telling my story in such a historic and unprecedented time.

I would be a tad bit delusional to attribute my success to just one person or event. I want to thank my family, teachers, professors, colleagues, and friends, who have all made me into the person I have become. Special thanks to my family; I love you all. To my fraternity brothers of Kappa Alpha Psi, because of you anything is possible. To my teachers and professors, thanks for never giving up on me; you truly make a difference. And to my friends and family, who contribute every day to my life and living experience in each of your own unique ways. I appreciate you.

About the Author

© Adam Fenster

Richard Antoine White began his tuba studies at the Baltimore School for the Performing Arts, where he graduated with honors. He went on to receive his bachelor's degree at the Peabody Conservatory of Music and his master's and doctoral degrees at Indiana University. Dr. White was principal tubist of the New Mexico Symphony Orchestra from 2004 until its untimely demise in 2011. He is now principal tubist of the Santa Fe Symphony and is in his tenth season as principal tubist of the New Mexico Philharmonic. He enjoys teaching at the University of New Mexico, where he is a professor of tuba/euphonium.